No Turning Back

A Witness to Mercy

Fr. Donald Calloway, MIC

www.fathercalloway.com

Available from:
Marian Helpers Center
Stockbridge, MA 01263

Prayerline: 1-800-804-3823
Orderline: 1-800-462-7426
Websites: www.fathercalloway.com
www.marian.org

Imprimi Potest:
Very Rev. Daniel Cambra, MIC
Provincial Superior
May 26, 2009

Library of Congress Catalog Number: 2009932587
ISBN: 978-1-59614-210-7

First edition (4th printing): 2010

Cover Photo taken by Ileana E. Salazar at Imperial Beach, California
Design by Kathy Szpak
Editing and Proofreading: David Came and Andrew Leeco

Acknowledgements:
Marian Fathers of the Immaculate Conception of the B.V.M.,
Terry Barber, Jason Zasky, Gina Shultis, Ileana E. Salazar,
Teresa de Jesus Macias (Mamita), Anne Velasco-Castro

Printed in the United States of America

MARIAN PRESS
STOCKBRIDGE MA 01263

2010

*Dedicated to
Mom, Dad, and Matt*

TABLE OF CONTENTS

INTRODUCTION

WHEN I WAS A TEENAGER, if someone had told me I would one day be a Roman Catholic priest writing a book about my life and telling the remarkable story of my conversion to people around the world — I would have said, "You're crazy ... ! I'm going to smoke a joint. Now get out of my face." Even today, it still amazes me that I'm a priest.

What you are about to read is the story of my conversion — what Jesus and Mary have done to my life, bringing me out of darkness and atheism to the fullness of truth in the One, Holy, Catholic, and Apostolic Church. And the conversion story is ongoing. Even today, I find myself in the midst of this mystery that God has called me into. In so many ways, I am not worthy. But by the grace of God — by His mercy — I continue to experience conversion every day.

Some may find the following story — my life story — to be almost unbelievable. After I give my conversion witness at conferences, it's not unheard of for someone to approach me and say, "I can't believe it. I think this is unbelievable." That's why whenever I do a speaking engagement, I always bring along a photograph of myself — a picture of what I looked like when I was in my late teens. Rest assured, I don't carry around an old photo because I'm an egomaniac. I do it so people can visualize what an *animal* I was before my conversion.

I don't necessarily blame people for being skeptical. If I were in someone else's shoes, I would probably have doubts myself. How is this possible? Is this story true? Because these kinds of events only happen in the Bible.

But when these same skeptics see my picture, they usually find it to be pretty powerful. My eyes are vacant and hollow, my skin is ashen, my malnourished body is gaunt and frail —

all physical manifestations of severe drug and alcohol abuse. It's a portrait of a haggard, out-of-shape, high school dropout with waist-length hair, an earring, and a Grateful Dead tattoo, not to mention the posture of the Shaggy character from *ScoobyDoo*. In the photo, I look like the personification of death. In truth, I am lucky to be alive.

When I was a teenager, my becoming a priest was the last thing anyone would have expected — especially my parents and closest friends. Besides the obvious problem that I was an angry misfit, I had no understanding of God. I had no respect for anyone or anything associated with religion. I was so ignorant of Christianity that I had never even *heard* of the Virgin Mary. Worse, I disdained Catholicism and laughed at those who practiced it — just as one might snicker about the practices and rituals of a bizarre cult.

In fact, I remember one Christmas when I used the Nativity scene in the neighbors' yard for target practice, plinking them with pellets from my bb gun. And then there was the time when a man called my parents' home and referred to himself as "Father." I didn't know what this meant, so when I answered the phone I said, "Father?" He said, "I'm a Catholic priest. Can I speak with your mother, please?"

I cussed him out, unleashing a stream of expletives — words that I cannot even repeat now — before hanging up on him. My parents had recently converted, and I assumed he was the one responsible for them getting mixed up with this God lie called Catholicism. My mother came running down the hall crying and screaming at me to stop cursing at him, but I didn't care. As you will see, my life was the farthest thing from everything that was good, true, and beautiful.

For those of you who can identify with this type of behavior, my experience proves that there is always hope, even for the worst of the worst. You see this is not just my story — this is important to emphasize — it's also a story bound up with God's faithful people. When I travel around the world to give my witness — the testimony of my conversion — I always tell the audience that they, too, are a part of my story. Often times, they respond by asking me, "How is that? We've never known you. And we certainly didn't know you when you were going through your rebellious years or your conversion."

I tell them as members of the Body of Christ, the prayers they pray for the conversion of sinners — well, those prayers really work. I am "Exhibit A"— evidence that when people pray, even for people they don't know — miracles can happen. Divine Mercy is for real!

That is why this is not only my story but also the story of a God who is so in love with His people. He listens to and answers their prayers. In these very difficult times, He is literally willing to raise up a bum like myself — someone who wanted to be nothing but a surfing hippie — and to change his life through the intercession of the Virgin Mary.

In writing this book about my life, I am asking the people who read it to continue to pray for me. Having experienced so much mercy and so many graces, I now have a great responsibility to be faithful and to proclaim the message that is the Gospel. As a priest, my role is to proclaim the truth; to be a victim, and to die to myself. That's why I'm a priest. I hope that to the end, like St. Paul, I will be found faithful — that I will run the course to its completion and win the prize.

I need to emphasize that this is not my own message. The Lord has called me to the priesthood so that I can proclaim His message and His saving truth — not adding anything to it, not subtracting anything from it. Today that is a challenge because there are many instances where people want to change the Gospel. They simply find it hard to live or find it difficult because they have been living in a certain pattern of sin.

Be warned: This book will fully expose the sinful side of my former life of which I remain very ashamed. Please understand that I don't recount my past to boast of all the sinful things I did or to appear to be a great sinner. I do it because I need to illustrate the totality and depth of the darkness I was in, so that the full glory and power of God's grace and mercy — especially through the intercession of the Virgin Mary — can be manifested.

For the sake of privacy, I have changed many of the names and places from my past. There is no sense in making old friends or acquaintances a part of this, lest they feel offended or prefer to let bygones be bygones. As for my behavior, I beg their forgiveness and also the collective forgiveness of the reader. It is only by making a "full confession" in this book that what has happened in my life can be fully understood, demonstrating what it is that God is willing to do in the life of a sinner.

Fr. Donald H. Calloway, MIC, STL
Steubenville, Ohio

1

ANIMAL

THE DAY I WAS CAPTURED IN JAPAN was straight out of a big-budget action film. One can easily picture the scene; it was just like the climax of a Hollywood movie. Imagine undercover agents, police officers, and American military police surreptitiously stalking a pair of hardened, young criminals, hoping to catch them in the act of delivering money and illegal drugs. What the criminals don't know is that the agents have used wiretaps to monitor their lines of communication and "turn" one of their associates, who has reluctantly agreed to lure the kingpin of the bad guys into a trap.

The tension builds as the good guys close in, even as they debate the pros and cons of confronting the criminals in a busy public place. The bad guys have insisted on meeting their associate — the traitor — in a train station, so that any attempt at capture is sure to compromise the safety of innocent bystanders.

Still, the good guys know this is their best and perhaps only chance to apprehend their targets, so at an opportune moment, they suddenly make their move. The criminals immediately realize they've been duped and do everything possible to resist. A violent struggle ensues, fists fly as bewildered commuters flee the area.

Naturally, the good guys don't win out right away. Before long, one of the suspects manages to escape the clutches of his pursuers. Then there's an extended chase, on foot, through the streets of a big city. Tires squeal as commuters slam on their brakes to avoid the reckless criminal, who purposefully runs into traffic in an effort to evade his pursuers. Shocked pedestrians duck aside as they see and hear men yelling and running in their direction. Those unlucky pedestrians who aren't paying attention or quick enough to get out of the way are knocked to the ground during the pursuit. Of course, in the end, the bad guys are apprehended and arrested, and the good guys gloat about their conquest, taunting the criminals as they take out their frustrations by roughing them up a little.

While this might sound like a stereotypical movie action scene, it was perfectly real. I was one of the bad guys in this scenario, chased through the streets by a multinational group of law enforcement officers. I was the so-called "big fish" that everyone was looking to capture, and by the time I was in handcuffs, the American and Japanese governments had already negotiated the terms by which I'd be released into the custody of the American military. Within days, I would be deported from Japan, on my way back to the United States where I would be confined to an institution. I was just 15 years old.

The plans for that fateful day were made over the phone the night before. As I remember it, I called my friend Nathan, who agreed to rendezvous with my friend Tommy and me — my main partner-in-crime — at one of the larger train stations in Yokohama, a major city roughly 18 miles southwest of Tokyo. The plan was to give Nathan my overflow cash — a little more than two million Yen — most of which I had recently stolen from local department stores. Then, Tommy and I planned to take him out on the town and blow the rest of the newfound money on alcohol, drugs, and girls — just as we had always done.

The morning of our capture Tommy and I were dressed in our typical garb, which instantly pegged us as your stereotypical mid-1980s, heavy-metal fans. I wore my favorite blue-and-black, tie-dyed pants and a Van Halen 1984 shirt, which featured the now infamous image of a blond, blue-eyed baby with angel wings smoking a cigarette. Tommy was wearing ripped, black pants and a ratty old Iron Maiden concert T-shirt with "The Number of the Beast" artwork on the front and "Beast on the Road" tour dates on the back. We both had long, messy hair — mine straight and dark, Tommy's curly and light, almost like a blond Afro.

I was about to give Nathan the equivalent of 10 thousand U.S. dollars, but even that large a sum of money didn't mean much to me. As was often the case, I had so much cash on my person that I could barely carry it around. The pockets of my pants — which had an almost absurd number of zippered pockets — were bulging with cash.

It had become my custom that when I accumulated more than I could carry around, I would call up a friend and turn the money over to him. It's not like I was being generous or a good friend. On the contrary, it's just that carrying around a backpack full of money got to be a real drag after a while. Being a minor, I didn't have a bank account or a permanent home where I could stash my belongings, so giving away the money was the next best thing. Anyway, if I needed more cash, I would simply steal more. Most of the time stealing in Japan was as easy as taking candy from a baby.

When Tommy and I arrived at the station, morning rush hour was over, but the station was still bustling with businessmen making their way to work. I had deliberately insisted on a 10 a.m. meeting time, hoping that most of the people unfortunate enough to have to actually work for a living would already be at their offices, slaving away at their jobs. That way, if for any reason Tommy and I needed to beat a hasty retreat, there would be fewer commuters clogging up our escape route.

I had already learned from experience that formulating a contingency plan was an important consideration in a situation like this, even if trouble seemed an unlikely possibility. Congestion is a major issue in Japanese train stations, as it is in almost every urban area in Japan. Imagine rush hour at New York City's Grand Central Station. Then imagine three times as many people in the same amount of space. That gives you an idea of how cramped and crowded it can be at Yokohama's train stations.

Another difference between Yokohama and an American station like Grand Central is that in Yokohama the tracks run through the lobby on either side, right next to where tickets and newspapers and comics are sold. Naturally, with so many people standing in such close proximity to the tracks, accidents are common. People frequently fall or get pushed onto the tracks when people are jostling for position, usually just as a train is entering the station.

Onboard the trains, the congestion problem is magnified further. In order to maximize every inch of space, railroad workers stand on the platforms and literally herd passengers into the cars — pushing, prodding, and stuffing them in, even as the doors are closing. This vaguely resembles a ranch hand herding sheep or cattle. Needless to say, those prone to claustrophobia find another way to get to work.

Once the doors close, things can really get interesting. It's often packed so tight inside that you can barely move. Groping is an everyday occurrence. Needless to say, taking public transportation in Japan is a crowded, smelly experience, especially during the warm-weather months.

Of course, I don't mean to suggest that taking the train in Japan is an entirely negative experience. For one thing, the stations are usually spotless, in spite of the heavy foot traffic. Those same workers that shepherd passengers into the cars double as janitors, wiping down benches and picking up trash whenever they get a free moment.

The passengers are generally fanatical about cleanliness, too. Many wear surgical masks over their mouths and bright-white gloves on their hands — the kind of gloves a doorman might wear at a fancy American hotel. At first, foreign visitors find the masks and gloves disconcerting and wonder, "Am I breathing or touching something I shouldn't?" But one soon learns that the Japanese are just making their best effort to stay germ-free, in spite of constant and unnaturally close encounters with lots of strangers.

But the best thing about the trains in Japan is that they almost always run on time. The Japanese are so regimented and committed to routine that not even a grisly train accident involving a commuter is enough to disturb the schedule. If a train is scheduled to leave at a certain time, you can almost set your watch by it. Oh, and the bullet trains go really, really fast.

I was hoping there would be fewer people inside the station when Tommy and I arrived, and everything did look normal as we made our way into the main lobby. The long, thin passageway had automated ticket machines and tracks on either side, with countless worker drones dressed in gray conservative suits passing us by. Others stood in line waiting to buy tickets from the ticket machines. Still others sat on benches reading the paper or comic books — phonebook-sized tomes called shojo comics that are published on a daily basis and extremely popular among adults.

I scanned the lobby, looking for Nathan's distinctive American features — frizzy, long hair and casual dress, which would stand out amidst the buttoned-down, close-shorn Japanese businessmen. It wasn't long before Tommy and I made visual contact with Nathan. I was just about to raise my arm and give Nathan a wave when a group of men who had been sitting nearby — with open newspapers obscuring their faces — suddenly jumped up, dropped their papers on the floor, and converged on me. I didn't know it at the time, but they were undercover Japanese police officers disguised as businessmen.

Before I could make a move, a group of a half-dozen officers piled on top of me in haphazard fashion. A short distance away, another group of a half-dozen men pinned Tommy to the floor. As this was happening, I caught a glimpse of Nathan running towards us, screaming, "Sorry, dude! Sorry! Oh, man, I'm sorry!"

I couldn't believe that Nathan had allowed the police to use him as bait to catch me. I wondered why he was helping the Japanese police. Nathan didn't even speak Japanese. How did he get hooked up with them?

I felt like an idiot for having been duped. And it wasn't often that I felt this way. I was vaguely aware that the U.S. military and Japanese government might have an interest in trying to hunt me down. I even considered the possibility that the U.S. Navy might begin listening in on any phone calls I made to my friends — military dependents who lived on Navy property. But I was pretty confident that none of my buddies would cooperate with the authorities. I wanted to beat the daylights out of Nathan for betraying me.

Two months earlier, Tommy and I had been living with our parents at Atsugi Naval Air Station — an airfield and supply center for U.S. military operations in Atsugi, Japan, about 20 miles from downtown Tokyo — where our fathers were both employed. As the son of a naval officer, I had lived a comfortable existence on the base, yet parental authority and military culture were decidedly at odds with my nature. As for Tommy, his father was a SEABEE, a handyman for the Naval Construction Force. Tommy wasn't quite as rebellious as I, but he had a terrible relationship with his parents, especially his father.

One night Tommy and I were totally wasted on *Shochu* (Japanese vodka), and we started railing against our parents. Typical teenage stuff: We were sick of going to school. We were sick of obeying everybody else's rules. We were sick of getting yelled at. All we really wanted to do was get drunk or high, listen to music, go surfing, and hang out with our girlfriends. What else was there to life, anyway?

Being very impetuous and off-the-cuff, Tommy suggested that we run away from home. He wasn't suggesting that we run away for a few days. He thought we should make a clean and permanent break with our families, and it didn't take much for Tommy to sell me on the idea. Always very smooth with the ladies, Tommy said he knew a Japanese girl who could put us up at her house for a few days. Once we were there, we could figure out our next move. That turned out to be the extent of our advance planning. We didn't even consider how we would get ourselves to this girl's house, much less what we were going to do for money or how we were going to support ourselves. We walked off the military base expecting to make our own way on the island of Honshu, the largest of the more than 3,000 islands that make up the country of Japan.

Neither of us said goodbye to our parents. Neither of us left a note or gave any indication if or when we were coming back. We didn't even take any money or any of our personal belongings, just the clothes on our backs. It was a pretty bold and cold thing for a pair of 15-year-olds to do. Looking back, it was also completely crazy. What on earth were we thinking?

Although I had made up my mind never to speak with my parents again, I was determined to stay in touch with my friends at Atsugi. So as soon as we got hooked up with the girls and drugs, I began phoning friends to regale them with stories about our crazy adventures. As was the case with Nathan, sometimes I even invited them out to meet Tommy and me somewhere, just to show off and give them a taste of the wild lifestyle we were experiencing. And to give them a big pile of money, of course.

But the Navy — not to mention my friend's parents — began to get suspicious when questionable characters like Nathan left the base empty-handed and inexplicably returned with wads of cash or armfuls of stolen merchandise, especially guitars and surfboards. Initially, the Navy didn't bother to take action, but when the Japanese government began to pressure them to get us under control, they realized that they would need to remove us from the Japanese community. That was easier said than done though, because Tommy and I roamed all over Honshu, changing location on an almost daily basis. The Navy soon realized that it was going to take a concerted effort to determine our whereabouts, so they would have to work in conjunction with Japanese authorities, using sophisticated surveillance techniques.

Looking back, I'm still surprised Tommy and I managed to elude law enforcement for such an extended period. Being in a foreign country without a legitimate occupation and scant knowledge of the native language — the only Japanese words I knew were the "bad ones" — crime was the only means we had to support ourselves. We started with petty crimes like stealing women's purses and grabbing money out of cash registers, but it wasn't long, a few weeks perhaps, before we ended up getting involved with a gang.

Not surprisingly, the Japanese gang immediately took a liking to both of us. We were Americans who thumbed our noses at authority and wanted nothing more than to live the gang's fast-paced lifestyle and experience all the wildness they were involved in.

Even more thrilling was that the girls who hung out with the gang were also very fond of us. They regarded us as a novelty and amused themselves by asking us to speak Japanese — giggling and laughing at us because our pronunciation sounded so funny to them. Over and over, they would ask us to utter simple phrases, things like, "What time is it?" or "Good morning" or "Hello, my name is ... ." Of course, like any adolescent boys, we enjoyed the attention. We were happy to indulge the girls, even if we were making fools of ourselves.

Meanwhile, committing crimes with members of the gang — mostly stealing from retail stores and running money to and from game rooms — seemed like a viable way of sustaining ourselves in Japan. Even if it seemed a little dangerous at times, it was hard for a teenaged boy to resist the perks. Music and drugs were everywhere, and their girls were extremely beautiful. Being fawned upon by 18- to 25-year-old babes made us feel like studs.

Under the tutelage of the members of the gang, Tommy and I were soon committing crimes that would be considered felonies in the United States. By day, we would scope out stores, looking for the easiest targets. Gaining access to stores in Japan is much simpler than stealing from the locked-down, alarm-protected businesses in America. Maybe things have changed in recent years, but at the time, it wasn't uncommon for Japanese merchants to leave their establishments unlocked at night. Instead of depositing their daily cash receipts in the bank, some shopkeepers kept the money in a box directly below the cash register in anticipation of the next day's opening.

At night, we would return to our chosen marks, either sneaking or breaking in to take whatever we wanted. We stole everything from amplifiers and electric guitars to skateboards, surfboards, and mopeds. Sometimes we were so brazen that we would rob a store during business hours, tucking whatever we could carry under our trench coats before walking out the door.

The only problem is when two Caucasian boys are seen running from a crime scene in Japan and hundreds of thousands, or even millions, of Yen are missing, it's very obvious who is responsible. When it happens on an everyday basis, it becomes an international incident.

That explains why the Japanese wanted us out of their country — dead or alive, it didn't matter to them which — and they wanted us out fast. Years of bad behavior by U.S. servicemen had made the government especially sensitive to any criminal activity that could be connected with the U.S. military.

In fact, it wasn't all that unusual to find a throng of Japanese citizens assembled outside the gates of the Air Station to demonstrate their disapproval of the behavior of American servicemen. But this was worse because we weren't even servicemen; we were the *children* of servicemen. The Japanese thought it absurd that the American military couldn't somehow keep us under control. Naturally, it wasn't long before the Navy regarded us as nothing more than an embarrassing diplomatic nuisance. Makes sense that my favorite song during this time was Bon Jovi's "Wanted: Dead or Alive."

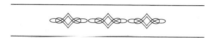

When the Japanese officers rushed in, it felt like the entire train station suddenly converged on me, like I had become the center of a black hole. Within seconds, a mass of humanity was on top of me, almost taking my breath away. Some guys in my position might have panicked, but I retained my composure and focused on what I needed to do to escape. Luckily for me, the police underestimated my ability to weasel out of tight situations and didn't coordinate their efforts. Instead of sending two men in to tackle me — leaving the rest to form a perimeter — all six men immediately piled on, perhaps assuming that the sheer weight of their bodies would be enough to keep me down. But I was as slippery as butter and began to finagle my way out of the pile.

Tommy wasn't nearly as elusive. When the police jumped him, they quickly managed to pin both of his arms and legs to the floor. "Dude, run!" I heard him yell as I squirmed free. As I was getting up, I noticed someone out of the corner of my eye that I hadn't seen earlier — my dad. He didn't make a move towards me. He was quietly watching the whole scene unfold at a distance.

I heard Japanese voices yelling behind me as I bolted out of the station and made my way out into the street. I don't know what they were yelling, but they sounded angry, probably because they were embarrassed about letting a scrawny American boy escape their grasp. Or maybe it was because I left them on top of each other in a heap, as if they were playing chumps in a comedy routine.

As soon as I busted through the station doors, I ran right into traffic, figuring the officers wouldn't be willing to risk their lives chasing a seemingly suicidal teenager down the middle of a crowded street, where they'd have to negotiate a mix of onrushing cars, bikes, and mopeds. While the streets in Japan aren't as wide as they are in the United States, this was a major thoroughfare — equivalent to an American road with two lanes running in each direction. Basically, I started playing a real-life version of the video game "Frogger," trying to make my way across the screen, er, street without getting killed. I would try to go forward, but then I'd have to jump back to dodge a speeding two-wheeler. Then I'd start moving forward again.

Ironically, I was more concerned about being hit by a moped or bicycle than I was by a car. In Yokohama, the streets are so congested — even at mid-morning — that mopeds or bicycles will often be traveling faster than cars, since they can weave in and out of traffic. And since the traffic laws in Japan are loosely enforced and only loosely observed, no one seemed compelled to yield. It was my responsibility to stay out of harm's way.

As soon as I got to the other side of this main thorough-fare, I started running along the sidewalk, stores flashing by as I dodged pedestrians. To my surprise, the cops remained hot on my tail. Being that I was young, fast, and nimble — not to mention that I had plenty of experience at running from law enforcement — I thought I had a good chance of getting away. But these men didn't give up easily. Then before long my diminished lung capacity — which could be attributed to all the cigarettes and marijuana I smoked — began to take its toll. The police officers continued to yell in Japanese — probably something along the lines of, "Stop that kid!" But nobody tried to trip me or knock me down, although I bowled over a few senior citizens who got in my way. By the time they heard the police officers' orders, I was almost past them already.

When I realized I might not be able to escape, I unzipped my pants pockets and began discretely dropping wads of cash on the ground. I figured if I was going to get busted, it would be best if I didn't have to explain how I managed to get my hands on several million Yen. I also hoped that bystanders would scramble to pick up the money, creating another obstacle for my pursuers to negotiate. Handful after handful of money I threw to the ground. I have no idea what happened to any of it, but I'm sure a few people came away feeling like they had just won the lottery.

Meanwhile, I made my way towards an open-air market — one filled with outdoor clothing and shoe stores. My rationale was that it might be easier to lose my pursuers by running *through* stores filled with shoppers, rather than simply running up and down the streets. Perhaps I could get lost among the racks of suits or skirts, instead of having to outrun the police over a long distance. But by the time I ran into an outdoor jean shop, I was really beginning to get scared. These guys were determined to catch me and were obviously in good shape. At this point, I was really breathing hard and beginning to wheeze audibly, like an asthmatic suffering a bad asthma attack.

My pace got slower and slower, and then suddenly I felt someone grab hold of my hair, getting enough of a handful to use it to drag me to the ground. I heard the man say, "We caught you, you little punk!" For the first time, I noticed that American military policemen (MPs) had also been chasing me.

Immediately, I tried to get up off the ground and even took a half-hearted swing at the MP who caught me. But he was so big — about six-foot-three, no neck, with arms thicker than my thighs — that he could easily hold me at arm's length. The other American MPs began calling me names and telling me how I was going to be locked up. One of them screamed at me, "Do you know what you've done? Do you know what you've done?" I spit at him and told him off.

As one might expect, the MPs quickly got tired of taking my abuse. One of them pulled my right arm up behind my back in an arm lock, as police officers are taught to do when apprehending a suspect. They knew they were hurting me because I let out a blood-curdling scream, yet they didn't let up. Then as they forced me to the ground, one MP put his knee on my neck and pressed my face into the cement. Even while they were putting on the handcuffs, I continued screaming obscenities. I knew I couldn't take on any of these guys in a fight, but I didn't want to let them know they were intimidating me.

It was a long ride back to Atsugi, at least an hour. Tommy was transported back to the base with me, although he was in a different vehicle. During the trip, I felt like an animal trapped in a cage. All I could think about was escaping. The fact that my dad was now in the car with me certainly didn't make me feel any better. He didn't say anything, but if he had, I would have cursed at him, just like I cursed at the policemen. I hated everybody at that point. I just thought, "This really sucks." In my mind, this was yet another case of authority inconveniently getting in my way and taking away my freedom.

When we finally got back to the base, they immediately threw me in the brig, a 10' x 8' cell furnished only with a little cot. There was no sink, no toilet, no reading material — nothing to do but vent. One of the MPs assigned to guard me — a Filipino-American — was especially abusive, seeming to take great pleasure in calling me names. Of course, I was in no mood to take any garbage from anyone. So I started spitting on him and called him derogatory names. Then I said, "If I ever get out of here, I'm going to kill you!" His fellow guards ushered him down the hall in an effort to prevent the confrontation from escalating any further. That was fine by me. I couldn't stand to look at him any longer.

After a while, another MP came to my cell and advised me I was going to be deported from Japan as soon as possible. He said that the American military had already made the arrangements with the Japanese government. Being that I was still a minor and hadn't committed any capital offenses, the Japanese had agreed not to press charges for any of my assorted crimes, provided that I return immediately to the United States and enter into an institution for treatment. Oh, and my parents would have to compensate countless individuals for the merchandise I had stolen — all the thefts that could definitely be traced to me.

When I heard I was about to be kicked out of Japan, my motivation to escape was redoubled. The first few months I lived in Japan, I had hated my new home with a passion. But after a while, I grew to like it. Japan had drugs and girls, beaches and booze, just like the United States, and it was much easier to steal money over there. Now I even had a "girlfriend" — maybe not a girlfriend in the traditional sense of the word —but a "friends with benefits" arrangement.

But now the life I had created for myself was in jeopardy. As an opportunist, I had always been able to quickly size up a situation to get what I wanted. Now I really needed to put those skills into action. I actively considered all the possible options and came to the conclusion that a fight-kick approach obviously wasn't going to work with the oversize gorillas who were guarding me. I had to get into a situation where I would have a chance to outrun the MPs, a situation where their size and heavy equipment would work against them.

Since there was no toilet in the brig, I asked for permission to use the nearest restroom. To my surprise, they took off my handcuffs and let me out of my cell. I walked down the hall towards the bathroom, but when I reached the door, I just kept going — running the rest of the way down the hall and out the door into the sunshine.

Of course, as soon as I split, the guards sounded the alarm and locked down the entire base. They shut the gates and effectively prevented me—and everyone else—from getting back out into the real world. I ran through the officers' housing and across the golf course, heading for a wooded area that offered several potentially good hiding places. But when I heard the sound of dogs barking behind me — aggressive Doberman Pinchers that were strong, intense, and had the speed and stamina to cover a lot of ground in a hurry — my options for escape were narrowing.

When I realized the dogs were hot on my trail, I knew I had to take desperate measures, so I stopped running and squeezed myself down into a sewer drain. On the positive side, jumping into the sewer kept me from being captured and kept the dogs from getting at me. Sure enough, shortly after I took the plunge, I saw police cars go by, their sirens wailing. Then came the dogs and the crackling sound of their handlers' walkie-talkies.

On the downside, I had voluntarily jumped into a pool of raw sewage. I tried not to look around too much, so I wouldn't get a good look at exactly what I was wading in. But it was hard to ignore the stench, which was so strong at times that I could barely keep from vomiting.

During the period of time I was in the drain, the sewage ebbed and flowed — at one point rising all the way up to my neckline. I was lucky it didn't rise any higher because I'm not sure I could have extricated myself. I had wedged myself so far down — and the walls of the drain were so slick — I probably couldn't have hauled myself up, even if it was a matter of life and death. I would have drowned in a pool of excrement.

Still, except for the brief moment when I thought I might be completely submerged, I never seriously contemplated getting out. I would have remained in that sewer drain as long as necessary if it would have saved me from being captured and deported.

Unfortunately, as time went on, I heard the sound of barking dogs again. Looking up out of the drain into the light, I saw an MP come into view, holding back a pair of madly barking Dobermans. The MP said, "Alright, come up out of there, son." I tried to lift myself out, but as I feared, I couldn't get out under my own power. Another MP had to squeeze in with me and literally drag me out. When he came down and made eye contact with me, he gave me the most disgusted look I've ever seen in my life, as if to say, "I can't believe it's because of you that I'm standing in a big pool of feces. This is not what I signed up for when I joined the Navy."

After the guards handcuffed me, they walked me all the way back to the brig — a 25- or 30- minute walk. I was so nasty and foul that they didn't want to soil the seats of their military police vehicle. Then, when we got back to the jail, they didn't even let me take a shower. An MP took me into the bathroom and sort of half-heartedly washed me down using a sponge and a slop bucket. It was clearly going to be a long night. Of course, having learned their lesson the hard way, now they didn't let me go to the bathroom by myself any more. When I used the restroom, an MP had to be there, to my chagrin and his, I'm sure.

Meanwhile, unbeknownst to me, my self-centered actions were affecting my entire family. Two weeks earlier, the American military directed my mother to leave the country with my younger brother, Matthew, ostensibly to begin resettling our family in the United States. The rationale was that my father and I would then have a place to come home to when they found me. Or in a worst-case scenario, the authorities would at least know where to ship my body. Before I was captured, the Japanese considered it more likely that I would be going home in a body bag. The Navy had already settled on Reading, Pennsylvania, as my father's next duty station where he would serve as a supply officer.

Meanwhile, my father stayed behind in Japan to help look for me, promising my mother that he wouldn't leave until he found me, and wouldn't return to her without me. In this respect, I was better off than Tommy, who was deported a day earlier (he didn't try to escape from the brig), but his mother and father had already abandoned him, having left for the United States before we were apprehended. I'm told he was sent to Texas, where his father relocated, but I've had no contact with him since the incident in the train station. It didn't really bother me that we lost touch. Like most of my so-called friends, Tommy was disposable. Once he was out of sight, I didn't give him a second thought.

The day after I was recaptured, my guards transported me over to Yokosuka, another U.S. military installation, where my dad and I were put on a military flight to Honolulu. From what I understand, there was no consideration given to putting me on a commercial flight. In fact, I was still so angry and defiant that they literally handcuffed me to the plane. We were transported on one of those C-130 cargo planes where there's cargo in the center and web seating on the sides. They strapped me in to a webbed seat and positioned an MP on both my left and right. Then they chained one of my legs to an MP and one of my arms to the fuselage.

It was certainly the prudent thing to do. My handlers knew I had absolutely no regard for life — not theirs, not even my own. They were convinced I would do something stupid to put everyone in harm's way. In a certain sense, they were right because I was, quite simply, out of my mind. It was ironic. When my family moved to Japan two-and-a-half years earlier, I had resisted the move. Now I didn't even want to return to the States.

Once we touched down in Honolulu, we had to walk through the length of the terminal to reach our connecting flight, which would be a commercial flight to Los Angeles International Airport, better known as LAX. With my feet shackled, I shuffled through the terminal, the intimidating-looking MPs still at my side. Although I was handcuffed, the MPs had neglected to gag me, so I screamed and shouted the most vile obscenities at any passersby who made eye contact. I was humiliated by the fact that everyone was staring and whispering. Judging by all the attention I was receiving, one might have thought I was a convicted serial killer.

Naturally, the guards kept telling me to be quiet, but it was no use. One of the MPs even made the silly mistake of trying to cover my mouth with his hand. Like an animal, I tried to bite him. Looking back on it, I can only imagine what my father must have been thinking as this surreal scene was unfolding. At the time, I couldn't have cared less.

As we boarded the connecting flight from Honolulu to LAX, I got more of the same stares and heard more of the same whispering that I heard in the terminal. Although I was still annoyed by it, I stopped fighting and venting my anger. It finally kicked in that I was a bad dude — that I was probably freaking out the other passengers. I'm sure they were thinking, "Who is this kid that he needs to be shackled, handcuffed, and chained to two policemen? And is it safe to be on an airplane with him?" Plus, I was so tired and disgusted at this point that I just didn't want to fight anymore. "Would you like chicken or beef, Sir?" asked the stewardess at one point. Whatever. I hadn't slept or had a shower in almost three days — since before the sewer experience — and I was feeling it. To say that I was nasty would be an understatement.

When we got off the plane at LAX, the MPs escorted me as far as the main terminal. One of them then turned to me and said: "Here's the deal. Your mother and brother are in Pennsylvania. As you know, your dad is here with you, and we are going to release you to him. Do you agree to go with him to see your mother and to enter into an institution? If so, we are going to take off your handcuffs."

My first thought was, "Idiots. If they take off the cuffs, I'm going to run." I had friends in southern California from a few years earlier and thought I might be able to track them down. And to go surfing again in SoCal would be awesome.

But what exactly was I going to do? Everyone I knew in southern California was also a military dependent. Since I hadn't stayed in touch with anyone since moving to Japan — that out-of-sight, out-of-mind thing again — I had no way of knowing if any of my friends were still living in the same place. Without money, transportation, or any particular place to go, my normally cocky bravado was cooled temporarily. The idea of making my own way in Los Angeles was a frightening enough prospect that I decided to stay put. I reluctantly agreed to the MPs' demands, and the guards went back the way they came. I boarded yet another plane with my father, this time en route to our final destination — Philadelphia, Pennsylvania.

It was on this long flight that I spoke with my father for the first time since running away from home. Like everyone else, I had cursed him out a few times since being captured, but this was the first time we had a somewhat civilized exchange of words. I don't remember what we talked about — and make no mistake, I'm sure I was still an arrogant jerk — but for the first time, we had some semblance of a conversation. I suppose a lot of awkward silence was better than total silence.

When we landed in Philadelphia, my mom was waiting for us at the gate. In those pre 9/11 days, friends and relatives could meet arriving passengers as soon as they exited the jet way. I knew she was going to be there, but I didn't really care. I was so tired and disgusted that all I cared about was having a place to crash.

Yet when we got off the plane, my mother rushed up to me, hugged me, and smothered me with kisses. She told me how happy she was to see me. It had been almost two-and-a-half months since I had last seen her, right before I ran away in Japan. She was so motherly, telling me how much she loved me. It didn't seem to bother her that I looked awful — disheveled, stooped over, my eyes vacant and cold. She even called me "Donnie," a name that only she used with me.

But something about the way she approached me got me really agitated again. When she tried to embrace me, I immediately pushed her away, pointed my index finger in her face, and said with the most hateful voice imaginable: "I hate your guts!"

And I meant it. It was years of teen rage and frustration wrapped up in a single statement and gesture. Of course, no mother could handle that kind of response from her first-born son. Right there in the terminal, my mother broke down. She snapped like a twig and started crying uncontrollably. I didn't care at all. I was as unfeeling as a rock.

My dad was furious about me talking to my mother that way. He said something like, "How dare you talk to your mother that way!" But somehow, in spite of my behavior, we all made it out to the airport parking lot together. When we got into the car, I demanded to know where we were going. My mother whispered, "You are going to a rehabilitation center in central Pennsylvania. It will be a chance for a new beginning."

A new beginning? "Yeah, right," I thought. All I said was, "Fine, it will get me away from you!"

2

MY ST.
MONICA

TWO HOURS LATER, MY PARENTS DROPPED ME OFF at what turned out to be a well-known rehabilitation center in rural Pennsylvania. As one might imagine, the departure was very bitter. I didn't even want to say goodbye. All I wanted was to see them drive away. At 15 years old, I had caused an international scene, been deported from a foreign country, and in the process abruptly uprooted my entire family. But I didn't care.

I remember passing through customs on the way out of Japan, my father looking on as a customs official stamped the Japanese equivalent of "rejected" in my passport. In later years, whenever I met a Japanese person in the airport, I would pull out my passport and ask them, "What does that stamp mean to you?" Usually, they would have a puzzled look on their face, most likely because they weren't even aware such a distinction existed.

Of course, for all intents and purposes, my parents had been rejected, too — forced to move back to the United States eight months ahead of schedule. But that meant absolutely nothing to me.

As usual, I was only interested in how things affected me. When my mom told me I was going to enter an institution, it didn't even register at first. But when she told me I would be entering a *rehab* facility, I nearly freaked out. In my mind, rehab was a dirty word. If a person needed to enter rehab, they really needed help. Surely that wasn't me?

I was doing exactly what I wanted to do. I didn't *want* to stop. I didn't want to change. I didn't even care if I lived to age 30, as long as I could live the craziest lifestyle possible while I was alive. I never thought about long-range plans like having children and a family. And I certainly didn't expect to live to an old age. It just wasn't going to happen for me. All I was concerned about was having fun and enjoying beautiful women.

Naturally, I resented the fact that the military and my parents were forcing me to enter a rehab facility. In my mind, they were oppressing me, choking me, taking away my freedom and everything that I loved doing — not looking out for my best interests. That's how I interpreted anyone who wanted to see me change.

I felt like I was the only one who had the courage to live life to its extreme. I was the only one who had an appropriate philosophy of life. I was the only one I knew who was "real."

As we were driving deep into the Pennsylvania woods heading to the rehab center, I vaguely recalled hearing stories from friends about survival school programs where they took "troubled" boys out into the woods and made men out of them. Was this the kind of place I was going to? My parents hadn't given me any clues as to what kind of place this would be.

Were they going to show me how to start a fire with two sticks? Or teach me which wild berries and mushrooms were safe to eat? Maybe they would demonstrate how to make a hunting knife out of river rocks? In my mind, I tried convincing myself that rehab might not be so terrible after all. My relatives in West Virginia had taught me plenty about hunting and fishing and living off the land. Spending a summer alone in the wilderness with nothing but a wool blanket, a poncho, a compass, and a water bottle? "Bring it on," I thought. Besides, any kind of rehab was better than living with my parents.

Anyway, it's not like I had a choice about where I was going. Unless I was going to run away again and bum up and down the Pennsylvania Turnpike, I didn't have any other options.

The other thing I pondered during the drive through Pennsylvania was my relationship with my family. For a 15-year-old kid, I certainly thought I knew a lot, but the one thing I couldn't fathom was where my family's love and concern came from.

My parents were worried sick about me the entire time I was on the run in Japan. But could you blame them if they had decided to disown me? It's not like I was calling home every night saying, "Hi, Mom. Just checking in. I pulled another heist today and made off with a million Yen. How was your day? Was the officers' wives club bake sale a success?" No, after I ran away from Atsugi, my parents were as good as dead to me. As far as I was concerned, I no longer had any affection for them and never wanted to see or speak to them again. And since I had no affection or love for them, it didn't cross my self-centered mind that they would love me in spite of my behavior.

If I had known about the turmoil I had caused those last few months in Japan, I might have been even more surprised about their dedication to me. Since I had no contact with my parents during the time I was on the run, I had no idea about the tension I had caused within my family. For almost two months, I was totally estranged from my father, mother, and brother Matthew. It wasn't just that I was missing and my family was worried about my personal welfare. As I alluded to earlier, the Japanese government was furious that the U.S. Navy couldn't control me, so they put pressure on our military to find and deport me as soon as possible.

I don't want to come across as being more troublesome than I actually was. Over the years, there have been several well-publicized incidents where U.S. sailors committed far more heinous crimes in Japan than I ever did, but let's just say I was obviously not a positive reflection on our military presence there. My behavior clearly didn't do my father's career any favors. The Navy had a very negative opinion of my behavior in Japan.

Still, in some ways, I think my father had an easier time dealing with my behavior than my mother. He could at least wrap himself up in the extensive responsibilities of being a Lt. Commander. His work might have been an inadequate distraction, but it was a distraction nonetheless. Plus, he wasn't my biological father; I took his name when he adopted me, shortly after marrying my mom. So there wasn't that added biological and heartfelt bond between us, or so I thought.

Meanwhile, my mother, LaChita, had a major maternal crisis. Although she also worked — teaching English as a second language in the Japanese community — that was hardly enough to soothe her heart and keep her mind occupied. In a word, she was crushed by my behavior. Thanks to me, she was a broken woman.

But God works in mysterious ways, and it turns out He did have a plan. During this period, my mom consulted with many different friends and acquaintances, looking for anyone who might be able to help her get through this incredibly stressful situation I had created for her. For whatever reason, there was an inordinate number of rebellious kids living at Atsugi, so many of the other military wives could identify — at least to some small degree — with my mother's situation.

Yet God's plan was actually set in motion by a Filipino woman named Anne who offered my mom the following providential advice: "I know what you have to do to solve your problems," she said. "What? I've tried everything," my mother pleaded. She said, "You have to talk to a Catholic priest. He will have the answers."

As an almost full-blooded Italian, my mother should have been a devout, Rosary-praying Catholic, yet she had had no experience with the Catholic Church since she was a little girl. For some reason, when my great-grandparents came to Ellis Island from southern Italy, they didn't teach Italian to their next generation of children nor did they pass on their Catholic faith. But my mom knew her roots were Catholic and even remembered back to a time when her grandmother had tried to impart the basics.

At any rate, she felt like she had nothing to lose by talking to a priest. One day she walked over to the chaplain's office at the Air Station. The priest listened patiently to her story and then began talking to her about the Catholic Church.

This priest began by chronicling the story of St. Monica and St. Augustine — a story that must have easily resonated within my mother. He told her how Augustine, the son of Monica, lived a rebellious and sinful life and ditched his mother, running away from her even as she sought him.

Augustine is famous for saying, "Lord, make me chaste, but not today." He was a sensual, radical man. He even had an out-of-wedlock affair with a woman and then had the audacity to name the child Adeodatus, which translates to "a gift from God."

Yet in spite of, or perhaps because of, Augustine's sinful and rebellious behavior, Monica cried night and day and prayed her heart out for his conversion. While my mother had no expectation that I would ever turn out even vaguely religious, she was comforted by the fact that Augustine did one day convert to Catholicism, become a Doctor of the

Church, and is now recognized as one of the greatest saints of all time.

The priest also told my mother about Mary — the mother of Jesus — and about her sorrows and the sword that pierced her heart. He told her about confession, the Eucharist, the Rosary, and the Holy Father — all the wonders and glories of Catholicism. My mother, describing this to me years later, said it all seemed so right and true. She felt at home and knew this was the answer to her problems. For the first time, my mother had hope, something to cling to that was beyond human wisdom.

Meanwhile, my mother wasn't the only one being introduced to Catholicism. My mom convinced my father to visit the chaplain, too. My father grew up in an Episcopalian household in Asheville, North Carolina. Even though he wasn't a devout Episcopalian, he did attend services on a regular basis. It wasn't a big leap for him to consider Catholicism. In fact, his boyhood church was High Anglican, and externally it looked very much like a Catholic church. Episcopalians even recite the same creed: "We believe in one God. ... We believe in one, holy, catholic, apostolic church."

Soon after my dad began going to Mass with my mom, he, too, realized they were meant to convert. And as he read more and more about Jesus and Mary, he, too, began to fall in love with Catholicism.

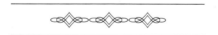

As for me, love of God and neighbor was about the last thing on my mind when we finally pulled up to the entrance of the rehabilitation center. I was all about hate. A few representatives of the center came out to greet us. They gave me the predictable "We're so glad you're here, we're so glad you came" routine. They were smiling, friendly, and upbeat. I was thinking to myself, "You people suck. You all suck. You're just playing a game for me."

After a few minutes of chit chat with the administrators, it was time for my parents to leave. Predictably, my mom tried to give me a hug, but I didn't hug her back. I just let my arms hang limply at my sides. As a result, my mom and dad turned and walked away in tears. I didn't wave or wish them well or anything. All I cared about was getting to my room and taking a shower. I still hadn't had a proper bath since being pulled out of the sewer, which at this point seemed like ages ago.

After I was brought to my room, I met my roommate, a 17-year-old high school dropout from Philadelphia who was really into drugs. Compared to him, I looked like a recreational user. But the most notable thing about my roommate was that he was totally obsessed with Led Zeppelin. He knew everything there was to know about the band and practically worshipped Robert Plant and John Bonham. Not only did he know every word to every song they ever recorded, he knew all kinds of obscure things about Jimmy Page's interest in the occult and the guitarist's connection to satanist Aleister Crowley.

After I filled him in on my situation, he was pretty much incredulous, just like everyone else at the center. He said, "Dude, you just got off a plane from Japan and you're coming *here?*" Most of the 70 or so guys and 40 or so girls at this place were from Pennsylvania or neighboring states, so my life story really helped me stand out from the crowd. I told my roommate about Japan, while he taught me about Zeppelin and classic rock.

But mostly the two of us had pity parties. I would pour my heart out about how much I missed Japan and all my friends. And then he would dump all his frustration and anger on me. We would talk into the wee hours of the morning, our conversations usually punctuated by things like, "That was really bad luck" or "That really sucks, man." It was pathetic, but it was comforting to have somebody affirm the things I was feeling. To my surprise, however, he had checked himself in voluntarily, a fact that was a little hard for me to believe.

Yes, my roommate and I were both messed up on drugs, but we weren't necessarily the typical patients. Many of the other teens in my building were seriously depressed, to the point where just getting out of bed in the morning was a challenge for them. Others were what you'd call cutters — kids who cut themselves with a knife or blade as a way of escaping from whatever pain it is they are fleeing from.

I spent most of the summer program trying to avoid the corny counseling sessions — referred to as "small group" — which I absolutely abhorred. To this day, whenever I hear the words "small group," I panic and my heart starts racing.

In these intimate settings, we were supposed to talk about our problems. Could you imagine me opening up to strangers about problems I didn't even think I had? For instance, the counselors would say, "What do you want to work on while you're here?" I was a total jerk, so I would sarcastically respond with something like, "I really want to stop biting my nails." In a disapproving tone, they would say, "That's not really why you're here." And I would fire back with, "Well, what do you want me here for? I really don't care about your stupid program."

Ironically, when I talked with a counselor one-on-one, I was, at times, willing to be open and forthcoming — especially if a cute, female counselor was involved. Then I was capable of being a little charmer. But in a group, I always felt like I had to impress the girls or act macho for the benefit of the guys. Of course, if I were forced into a one-on-one session with someone I didn't like, I would totally clam up. Then you would get nothing out of me.

At night, it was more of the same, except the atmosphere would become even more touchy-feely. The counselors would take us outside. We would sit around a campfire roasting marshmallows and sing peaceful songs like "Kumbaya" and "This Little Light of Mine." We would also sing Carole King's "You've Got a Friend." I was like, "Yeah, I've got a friend. It's called marijuana."

The dumbest thing, though, was when the counselors asked us to do New Age-type exercises where we were supposed to designate some object as our "higher power." For some guys, their higher power would be a tree or their guitar or some other inanimate object. But I had enough brains to know that an inanimate "higher power" wasn't going to help me or anyone else in the program. My response was, "You guys are losers. I'm on my own."

The only activities I really looked forward to were the outdoorsy sports like swimming, playing volleyball, or rock climbing. At least running around outside made some sense. I mean, if you're a parent with an immature child — and essentially the counselors were substitute parents for kids who were about as mature as rambunctious two-year-olds —what do you want the child to do? You want to keep him occupied and let him run back and forth until he's exhausted.

But what I hated most about rehab was when we did "team-building exercises," the kind of silliness where you fall backwards off a ledge and trust that your teammates will catch you. Trust someone else? Why? I knew the only person I really trusted was myself. Plus, in this context, the exercises, in my mind, were absurd. The patients at this rehab couldn't even look out for themselves, much less be part of a team.

The bottom line was I never had any intention of learning how to be sober or how to be chaste or how to improve my attitude. In some sense, the counselors' methods were heroic in that they tried all kinds of methods and techniques to help me. I just didn't want anything to do with them. They actually believed that they were going to help me get better by taking sugar out of my diet and feeding me natural fruits and vegetables. But my problem was not something that could be solved by adjusting my sugar intake or even walking me through a 12-step program. I didn't know this yet, but my problem was a deep wound within my soul. They offered me nothing but a band-aid.

At the time, I certainly wouldn't have acknowledged that there was a wound at all. Yet looking back on it now, I see that all the therapy they were trying was a secular approach to a problem that was very spiritual and deep. I had made up my mind that no matter what happened I didn't want to be there, and I didn't want to change.

Oddly enough, just as my parents were getting turned on to Catholicism, a few counselors at the center tried to turn me on to Evangelical Christianity. Technically, the counselors were forbidden from evangelizing, but it was obvious they were trying to influence me — and everyone else — in their own little ways.

The only problem was that these guys weren't exactly good Christian role models. I got very turned off by their proselytizing because they appeared to be living a double life. On the one hand, they were preaching to me about God and asking me to sing these dorky Christian songs. Yet when I would eavesdrop and listen to their private conversations, I heard them talking about the hips, butts, and breasts of the female counselors. They also idolized the same heavy metal bands I listened to.

I would say to them, "You call yourselves Christian?" They were hypocritical, and being the extremist that I was, I didn't want any part of that. Plus, Christianity just seemed like a dumb waste of time, something that could only get in the way of doing drugs and having fun. Ironically, the counselors managed to turn me even farther away from Christianity.

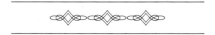

Meanwhile, my concerns in rehab were bigger than finding my higher power or heeding the advice of "Christian" counselors. One of the biggest obstacles I faced was obtaining drugs. The security measures made it almost impossible to smuggle in a bag of marijuana, but getting LSD was a realistic option. Since we were allowed to receive mail, friends on the outside could send letters, getting the LSD to us by dripping it on the back of the postage stamp. Then they would affix the stamp to the letter and mail it. When we received the letter, we would carefully remove the stamp and lick it to get high. We would lick the daylights out of those stamps.

It was funny because the counselors always boasted that no matter what we did, we would not be able to smuggle drugs into the facility. The counselors opened and read all the mail that the patients received, and they claimed to know all of the patients' drug smuggling tricks, yet those magic 33-cent stamps kept getting through. We used the same kinds of tricks that gang leaders use to manage their gangs from inside prison. A few patients even developed coded language to communicate with their druggie friends on the outside, but that was too much work for me.

Nevertheless, it wasn't as if I always had on-demand access to drugs. One time when no LSD was available, I was so desperate to get high that I tried smoking a banana peel. I had heard that if you coated the peel with toothpaste and let it dry out, you could smoke it and get a buzz. I saved a couple of banana peels, coated them with toothpaste, and then let them dry out in the sun on my windowsill. It didn't really do anything for me, but it sure was amusing trying to smoke a banana.

One day I used bananas for an even more devious purpose. The night before, I had watched the movie *Beverly Hills Cop*, which has a funny bit where Eddie Murphy (as Axel Foley) stuffs bananas in the tailpipe of a police car. In the scene, two undercover officers are staking out Foley's five-star hotel on Wilshire Boulevard. Realizing he is being tailed, Foley orders room service for the two officers and has the food delivered to them out on the street. While the police are sampling the cold poached salmon with dill sauce, Foley takes three bananas from the hotel's buffet plate, heads outside, and surreptitiously stuffs them into the car's tailpipe. Then Foley proceeds to drive off in a red Mercedes convertible. When the officers start their car and try to follow, it lurches forward a few feet, then sputters and dies in the middle of the road.

Feeling inspired, the next morning at breakfast, I lifted several bunches of bananas from the cafeteria. At lunchtime, I took my stash out to the employee parking lot and stuffed a couple bananas into the tail pipe of each of the counselors' cars.

A few hours later, when the counselors tried to leave for the evening, none of them could get their cars started, which predictably led to a "Great Meeting." They called all the patients into the main meeting room and started yelling, "Who did this? Who is responsible?" They threatened that unless the perpetrator voluntarily came forward, we would all be punished. But what were they going to do? Take away our pudding? Give us extra chores? It was kind of funny to watch them carrying on about bananas stuffed in tail pipes.

Naturally, I didn't confess, but the counselors discovered I was responsible. Someone ratted me out, it seems. So they sat me down and said, "Why would you do something like that? That's so cruel." After chewing me out, one of the administrators stated what was patently obvious: "You know, you really don't have a good attitude."

No kidding, I thought.

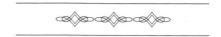

After spending about five or six weeks in rehab, I started to get more than a little stir crazy. Even LSD and the occasional prank wasn't enough to keep me placated. I just got so sick of the environment and relentless attempts at deprogramming that I decided to try to escape. My roommate and friends tried to talk me out of it. They said, "There's no way you're going to make it. We're way out in the sticks." I really had no idea where I was, and I vaguely recalled that it was a long drive through the woods to get there. But I felt there had to be a way out.

What I found was that it was remarkably easy to escape the grounds, as there weren't any guards on duty to keep the patients from walking out into the woods. On the other hand, the administrators knew that guards really weren't necessary. As I'd been warned, geography was the center's best defense mechanism. This place was so far out in the woods that I might as well have been trying to escape from Alcatraz or even Devil's Island. Without proper transportation, that is, a car, it was difficult just to find your way back to civilization. Still, I gave it my best shot. One morning I bolted and ran down the road — a long road — all the way to the nearest town.

Naturally, my decision to leave was spontaneous, so I wasn't quite prepared for the journey. Not only was my cardiopulmonary system still somewhat compromised from all the cigarettes and marijuana I had smoked in Japan, but I had neglected to take any food and water with me.

By the time I reached town, I was so thirsty and hungry that I made a beeline for the first (and only) store I saw, hoping to steal something to eat and drink.

Unfortunately, the proprietors of this country store watched me like a hawk from the moment I stepped inside, immediately making me out as an escaped patient. There was no other reason for a sweaty, funky, earring-wearing longhair to be in their store — way out in the middle of Pennsylvania farm country — unless he had escaped from the institution. I sure as heck didn't look like the son of a farmer. Anyway, it wasn't my kind of place. They sold canned goods and molasses. I was looking for Doritos and Mountain Dew.

Since I didn't feel like I could steal anything and get away with it, I walked out of the store empty-handed and began walking down a different road, one that I hoped would lead to yet another town. The cashier — who wore overalls and a John Deere baseball cap — must have dialed the rehab center as soon as I walked out the door. Heck, he probably had the number on speed dial.

About 20 minutes later, a van pulled up alongside me, and one of the counselors shouted, "Get in the van!" I yelled, "Kiss off!" before jumping over a cow fence and running off into a cow pasture. But the counselor was athletic and well rested, so it didn't take him terribly long to catch me. I didn't really resist. What was I going to do? All I said to him was, "You're going to take me back there? You suck!" He drove me all the way back, and I quietly finished out the last four weeks of the program.

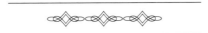

Before my "class" was discharged from the facility, the counselors made a token effort to prepare us for re-assimilation into society. Oddly, it was anything but an inspiring message. Basically, they said, "You're going to go back out in the world and only one of you is going to make it. The rest of you are going to relapse."

Say that again? This rehab center has an almost 100 percent failure rate? I'll bet they weren't highlighting that statistic in their marketing brochures. But it made me think, "What on earth am I doing here?" I sure wasn't going to be the one who made it. I didn't even want to be that one.

Naturally, after I was discharged I had nowhere to go, so I was forced to move in with my parents. It was an awkward situation as I hadn't seen or spoken to them in two-and-a-half months. At the rehab center, we were allowed to call our parents once a week, but I never did. Not once. When they gave me my weekly phone call, I would try to dial my friends in Japan. Of course, I never got through, because the phones weren't set up for international service.

Who knows, maybe my parents didn't want to talk to me when I was in rehab, anyway. Maybe they were relieved to get a break. After all, I was off the streets, under observation, and for the first time in a long time, they didn't have to worry about me getting into trouble with the law. Instead, my dad could concentrate on getting acclimated to his new post, my Mom could get the family settled in their new house, and my brother could get situated in his school.

What I didn't know is that during those two-and-a-half months, my parents had undergone their radical transformation. Shortly after my return from rehab, my mother said something so shocking that I didn't even know how to take it. She said, "Donnie, we have become Catholic."

My first impression was that they had joined a cult. Catholic? What is that? I really had no idea what that meant. She said, "We are Christian and we now go to church." I thought, "Great. Now my parents have bought into this stupid myth of God and have become so radical that they go to church every week."

I was supposed to be the one practicing extreme behavior. Now they were acting extreme, too, waking up at 7 o'clock in the morning, getting all dressed up, and going to church. Before they became Catholic, they would sleep in on Sundays or shop all day. Now they were waking me up at the break of dawn and asking if I wanted to go to church, too.

It was very noticeable how their lives had changed. My brother was now attending a Catholic school. Not only was my family going to church every week, they were praying before meals. I found it all so oppressive. Now I had to stop and wait for them to say a stupid prayer before I could eat. It all seemed to be too religious. Their house, in my opinion, had become a church.

Even the decorations in the house changed. There was a crucifix on the wall here and a statue there. Not only that, my mom was always putting prayer cards in my pockets or underneath my pillow. I would come home wasted after a night out with my friends, and after lying down, I would feel something under my pillow. At the time, I didn't know what it was, but it would be a prayer card with a funky dude on it with wings and a sword: St. Michael the Archangel.

Other times, I would reach in my pocket when I put my pants on in the morning, hoping to pull out a dollar or a pack of rolling papers. Instead, I would find a medal that read: "Mary, conceived without sin, pray for us." My mother was planting these little bugs to try and do something for me. Conversion by osmosis, I guess.

In the meantime, I just chalked my parents' actions up to bizarre behavior. I thought, "Fine. You live your little religious experience, and I'll just keep doing my own thing." Which I did. Little did I know that years later I would convert. But for now, things went from bad to worse.

3

FATHER
FIGURES

I'VE HAD THREE DIFFERENT last names in my lifetime. Each time my mother remarried, her new husband adopted me and I took his last name. Enduring a divorce, changing fathers, and getting a new surname is tough, but I will forever be grateful for the name "Calloway." You see, my biological father's last name is Crock.

I was born in 1972 when my mother, LaChita Bianco, was only 18 years old. In many ways, her childhood mirrored my own. She was born in northeastern Ohio, but when she was a young girl, her parents divorced. As a result, my mother stayed with her mother for some time before moving with her father to the remote locale of Wallace, West Virginia, where she grew up with her two brothers and two sisters.

As a young woman, my mother was exceptionally beautiful. She was petite with a dark complexion, which caused some people to mistake her for being Hispanic or even American Indian, owing to her long, jet-black hair and stunning looks. One might think a dark-skinned Italian would look out of place in north-central West Virginia, but the area is home to a sizeable Italian population. In fact, nearby Clarksburg — a small city of about 16,000 people located one-and-a-half hours south of Pittsburgh — is home to the annual West Virginia Italian Heritage Festival. Each summer since 1979, more than 100,000 people have come from as far away as Italy to celebrate the three-day event, which features authentic Italian cuisine and Italian-American entertainers like Tony Danza, Jo Dee Messina, Dion, and Fabian.

Still, it's undeniable that Wallace proper — which is populated by what I call "real West Virginians" — wasn't exactly the best place for a dark-skinned Italian girl to grow up. No offense to anyone who's from the Mountain State, but the whole hillbilly image that people conjure up when they think about West Virginians is somewhat true. People with suspenders, no shoes, missing teeth, and a gun — those are the kind of people who lived in Wallace and the surrounding area.

Needless to say, there wasn't much going on in this small, poor area. Consider my mom's home life: Her father's mountain house was built in a hollow way back in the woods — a spot nestled between two hills and shaded by a dense growth of trees. The closest neighbor was a half-mile down the road. The entire neighborhood even shared a party line — the same phone line.

It's hard to conceive of in this day and age when most teenagers have their own cell phone and pager, but if my mom wanted to call a friend, she had to pick up the phone in the living room and eavesdrop to see if anyone was already on the line. If not, she was free to make a call. If a neighbor was busy chatting away, she had to find out how long that neighbor planned to tie up the line.

Getting to school was no joy either. In order to get there, my mom had to walk to the end of the hollow, then take the bus to Clarksburg, a 30-minute commute, much of it over dusty dirt roads.

Considering that so few young people lived in Wallace, it was probably inevitable that my mom would eventually cross paths with the man who would become my biological father. My father, Donald, who was a few years older than my mother, lived in a hollow not far from my mother's house. But he was lucky enough to have a car — a souped-up hot-rod — which made his commute into town more tolerable. Shortly after they met, they fell in love and got married. On her wedding day, my mom was only 18 years old.

The two settled down together in West Virginia and, at first, seemed like a good match for each other. At that time, there was little work in the Clarksburg area, so they packed up and moved to Michigan. My father secured a high-paying job — by West Virginia standards, at least — in the unionized automobile industry in Dearborn, a suburb of Detroit.

Then as now, Dearborn is recognized as the center of the American automobile industry. The birthplace of Henry Ford, it remains home to the headquarters of Ford Motor Company. But Dearborn has also changed a lot in the past several decades. Today, it is also known for having the second-largest concentration of Arab-Americans in the United States, second only to New York City. In the early 1970s, however, Dearborn was predominantly white, and Ford was everything to the community.

Although my father's mechanical skills allowed him to earn more than enough to comfortably support his new family, moving to Michigan was a difficult adjustment for the Crock household. Both my parents were young and inexperienced — both in life and in the ways of a big city like Detroit. Prior to setting out for Dearborn, neither Mom nor Dad had much experience outside the small towns of Ohio and West Virginia. Plus, my dad's interests — hunting, fishing, and fixing cars — made him better suited to country living than city life.

Before long, my father began drinking heavily. Instead of saving money, he began squandering it on motorcycles, cars, and nights out on the town. After I was born, he began womanizing, spending more and more nights out with his friends instead of staying home with his family. My mother soon tired of his bad behavior, and while I was still an infant, they separated.

It turned out to be a very bitter divorce for the two young adults. After my father left, my mother tore up all the pictures she had of him and cut herself off from him completely. I wouldn't have a conversation with my biological father until I was 18 years old.

So much like my mother had done after her own parents divorced, I ended up going back to live on a farm in Wallace — under the care of my mother and grandfather. Except for the few times when my father would show up unannounced and incite heated verbal arguments with my mother, my memories of my early childhood are mostly good ones. I had a happy disposition and loved my mother very much.

As a young child, my mom and I had a very close relationship. I loved being with her more than anything else in the world. It would have been obvious to anyone who saw us together that we had a very strong bond. She was affectionate to me all the time. There was a lot of laughter and love to go around. I remember being proud of my mom, and I knew she was proud of me.

Of course, being so close in age it was easy to relate to her. Only 18 years apart, we loved the same music and same television shows. She would listen to eight-tracks of Neil Diamond, the Eagles, and Diana Ross, and I would bop right along with her.

One of her favorite pastimes was bowling. After she got home from the glass factory where she worked, she would take me along to the local alley. I vividly remember the way she would throw her sparkly, blue ball left-handed, letting it drift out towards the gutter before spinning back into the center, often knocking all the pins down in the process. To a little kid, her form and power were amazing. In contrast, all I could do was step up to the line, pull the ball back between my legs with both hands, and heave the ball. Naturally, my ball usually found the gutter long before reaching the pins, but that didn't matter to her. We didn't have much, but I remember that life was good and I was happy.

Although my biological father was absent while I was growing up, I did have several father figures in my life, most notably my grandfather and my uncle. Like my mother, my grandfather was very dark-skinned. One look and you knew he was either from southern Italy or an American Indian. No matter what season it was he always wore a flannel shirt, along with suspenders and worn-out jeans. He came across like a patriarch or a chief, a jovial, yet even-handed fellow who could be tough-as-nails when the occasion required it. He was definitely someone you didn't want to mess with.

To this little seven-year-old boy, he seemed larger than life, the kind of man one might see a grainy black-and-white picture of in a history book. He even carried himself like a noble warrior who'd been in battle, which made sense since he fought in the Korean War.

As a little kid, I loved spending time at his mountain house because everything seemed big and manly and had a strong, wild smell. In the morning, the aroma of bacon and coffee filled the air. Grandpa would send me out to the chicken coop to collect a basket of eggs. Then he would fresh-brew a pot of coffee, while he cooked up hearty portions of bacon and fried eggs.

At night, after Grandpa got back from tending to the fields and the animals, the mountain house took on a different smell. Before sitting down in his chair to smoke, Grandpa would make me caramel popcorn, which was my favorite treat. Then he would get out a cigar or his pipe and smoke cherry tobacco, filling the place with the rich, pungent smell of tobacco.

Meanwhile, his home was your typical outdoorsman's paradise. Grandpa had built the house himself, and the interior wood paneling gave each room a distinctive woody smell, the kind of odor that isn't evident in any "modern" home. The walls were decorated with the heads of deer, wild boar, pheasants, and black bears. Any wall space that wasn't filled by animal heads was occupied by rifle cases, shotguns, pistols, muzzle loaders, bows, and compound bows. Of course, he always had enough ammunition on hand to defend a small town.

As for the land itself, Grandpa owned many acres on which he grew everything from tomatoes and cabbage to corn. In addition, he owned about a dozen cows and kept horses and chickens. Naturally, Grandpa kept some of the farm's output for personal consumption, but he sold most of the produce on Interstate 50. He would drive his pickup truck west on I-50 to Parkersburg and sell produce right there at the Ohio state line. However, like most people in the area, he still had trouble making ends meet and would also collect state aid to supplement his income. Now that I think of it, most of my relatives were on state aid — either welfare or food stamps or both.

As I got older, Grandpa began demonstrating to me how to work the fields and raise animals. I have so many fond memories of those times. I loved to ride on the back of his John Deere tractor as he bailed hay. When I was very young, I couldn't help him much with the farm work, but at least I could keep him company. I'll never forget how much the hay would make my skin itch. I'd be scratching for hours.

Grandpa wasn't shy about exposing me to the harsh realities of life and death on a farm either. One time I was with him when he slaughtered one of his cows in the barn. The experience scared the daylights out of me. I remember him turning the cow around to face him and then putting a rifle to its forehead. Bang! It was surreal. I remember watching it like it was in slow motion. The cow fell to the ground in a heap. Then my grandfather calmly walked over, tied its hind legs together with a chain, and strung it up by the hocks.

There's nothing like the experience of seeing a cow strung up in your barn, blood and guts dripping. Yet Grandpa didn't seem at all put off by the wretched smell. He quietly removed the hide and then gutted its intestines. Soon there were just chunks of meat hanging there. I remember being in awe, like, "Wow, this man is my grandpa, and I want to be like him."

As I got older, Grandpa and my uncle also taught me how to hunt and how to fish — skills that have stuck with me to this day and remain a positive influence on my life. They would give me a small rifle like a .22 or a shotgun, and we would go out to hunt white-tailed deer, squirrel, and wild turkey. Or we would go out fishing for small-mouth bass or catfish. The walls of my grandpa's cabin were a testament to his skill as a hunter and fisherman.

As for my uncle, he was a lot like my grandfather, except he was younger and liked the same music that I enjoyed. One of my fondest early memories is coming back from a fishing trip in his Jeep — with the doors stripped off and just a roll cage. The wind was flowing through our hair as we listened to "Take the Long Way Home" by Supertramp.

To this day, I always say that if God hadn't called me to the priesthood, I would be living on either a farm or a beach. I do love farm life. I'm one of those strange people who doesn't mind smelling manure when driving through farm country. There is something paradoxically wholesome and pure about living on a dirty farm, and that feeling has always stuck with me.

While relatives like my uncle and my grandfather were both ideal role models when it came to manly activities like hunting and camping, I would be remiss if I didn't note the negative influence my environment had on my development.

As I got older, I encountered many men in the Wallace area who didn't set a particularly good example in how they treated, looked upon, and talked about women. I began to see that men didn't seem to have a deep-down respect for women. As far as I could tell, it was a man's job to go out and have a good time, consequences be damned. Over time, this attitude rubbed off on me. As a result, my model of what it meant to be a young man was clearly flawed from the very beginning. Some of my extended family members seemed to be particularly challenged when it came to affairs of the heart.

And while I wasn't conscious of it at the time, I also believe television, and later movies, played a role in shaping how I understood the world. You can probably guess the kind of television shows I enjoyed. I spent hours watching the World Wrestling Federation (WWF), *Rocky and Bullwinkle*, *Underdog*, *Starsky and Hutch*, *Grizzly Adams*, *Swiss Family Robinson*, and *BJ and the Bear*, not to mention Clint Eastwood movies and other spaghetti westerns. My favorite show was *The Dukes of Hazzard*, which aired on CBS on Friday nights. Watching Bo and Luke Duke ride around Hazzard in the General Lee, I began wondering about what it meant to be a man. But Daisy Duke and her denim cutoff short-shorts was the main attraction for me. She really captured my attention.

When I was around eight years old, my mother married a second time. This time she married a man who hailed from New Martinsville, West Virginia, a mid-sized town in Wetzel County on the West Virginia-Ohio border. I know that we lived right on the border between the two states because the Ohio River flowed right through our backyard. Ohio was just 100 yards away on the other side of the river.

Although our new home was a trailer home and nothing like Grandpa's, I still thought it was a cool place to live. For me, the main attraction was the trains. A set of tracks ran past the property, and I loved to stand near the tracks and watch the huge freight trains lumber past. Usually, they were transporting coal or chemicals, sometimes automobiles. The locomotive engineers would blow their horn for me as they passed by, always a thrilling experience for a little boy.

At the same time, I didn't enjoy living with my new dad. Even at the age of eight, I couldn't find much to like about the man. He was verbally abusive, not just to my mom and me, but to everyone. To make matters worse, he was a loafer, a heavy drinker, and so lazy that he couldn't seem to hold down a job.

I couldn't understand it, but no matter what my mom did it seemed she always had bad luck. You know, that old Ray Charles song, "If it wasn't for bad luck, I'd have no luck at all"? Well, that was my mom. She was such a good person but always seemed to get the short end of the stick when it came to relationships or jobs. It became clear that my new dad was either incapable or unwilling to provide for us. My mom did the only thing she knew she could do to take care of us. She decided to enlist in the Navy, which would guarantee us an income for several years to come. Unfortunately, it also meant she would have to leave me alone with my new dad for two months, while she went away to boot camp.

I remember it being a very traumatic time for me when my mother went off to boot camp in Florida. Not only was I losing my mom, I was losing my best friend. I was extremely close to her, and despite all the challenges she herself was experiencing, she was a loving and caring mother in every way.

The months that my mom was away at boot camp seemed like an eternity. I remember her sending me gift packages from Florida, with cards and toys and nice letters about how much she missed me. In particular, I remember receiving a toy Godzilla — the one where you pushed a button and the arm shot off. I thought it was the coolest toy I had ever seen.

On the other hand, my new living arrangement — two-plus months in a trailer home with my new dad — was far from ideal. I didn't necessarily mind the part about living in a trailer home; there's something about one that is kind of neat. I always liked when it would rain because of the sound the raindrops made on the roof. There's nothing like cuddling up on the couch in the living room of a trailer home — cartoons on the television set, a Dura flame log in the fireplace, and rain pelting the tin roof. It's a peaceful, snug feeling. I liked when I had that feeling because being around my new dad was anything but peaceful.

At best, my new father was very, very distant. He would often leave me home by myself for long periods of time. Then, when he was around, he was usually drunk, the kind of angry drunk that is very difficult to live with — especially for an eight-year-old boy who is missing his mother.

At home, I was always walking on eggshells, trying to avoid doing anything that might set him off. In order to get away from him, I spent a lot of time outside playing with my friends. But in a one-level trailer home, there's not a lot of space to avoid someone who's in a lousy mood. I counted the days until I would see my mom again.

Naturally, I was overjoyed when my mom finally returned home. Her return also marked the beginning of my experience as a military brat, a pattern of moving from one city to another, wherever my mom — and later my third father — happened to be stationed. But at the time, I didn't care where we moved to, as long as I could stay with her.

My mother's first duty station after basic training was in Norfolk, Virginia, and from a rural West Virginian's perspective, our new home city was a fascinating place. To outsiders, Norfolk is best known for having the world's largest naval installation, which serves as home port to more than 50 ships, including the World War II battleship *U.S.S. Wisconsin*. But for me, Norfolk was cool simply because it had a lot more people, traffic, business, and activity — not to mention more television stations — than I had ever experienced in West Virginia. Today, one can live virtually anywhere and still get literally hundreds of stations on satellite. But when we lived in Wallace, we could only tune in to CBS, NBC, and a handful of other stations on the VHF band.

Shortly after we settled in Norfolk, my parents' relationship took a turn for the worse. I remember them arguing and fighting virtually nonstop. There was tension over the fact that my mom was the breadwinner and also resentment because my dad never really wanted to leave West Virginia in the first place.

They separated and got a divorce when I was nine years old, and he moved back to New Martinsville. Once again, I found myself without a father. Only this time, I didn't have an uncle or grandfather around to fill the void.

It was around this time that I began to show signs of becoming a bad boy. Although I was only nine years old, I began telling little white lies and tried to smoke cigarettes. Of course, with Philip Morris based in Richmond, Virginia, tobacco is a huge industry in the area, so cigarettes were always easy to come by.

Like many of my friends at the time, I had a lot of freedom for a kid my age. Too much freedom, really. It's not that my mother didn't try to keep an eye on me. But as a single mom, she worked so many hours that when I was not in school, I was often with a babysitter. And when she came home from work, she was often too exhausted to pay much attention to me.

When I was nine, I got my first crush on a girl, which in a roundabout way, led me to begin stealing. Her name was Brandy, and she was cute as all get-out. We went to school together, and I wanted her to like me. So to win her over, I went to a local department store and stole a necklace. I just casually slipped it into my pocket and walked out the door. I remember the rush I got when I gave the necklace to her and she put it on: "Wow, she likes it!"

In two ways, that was a turning point for me. To begin with, that was the first time I had ever stolen anything. I knew stealing was wrong. Otherwise, I wouldn't have secretly slipped that necklace into my pocket. But I figured it was okay as long as I could get away with it. I mean, the guys on television always seemed to get away without getting caught. It was also a significant moment because I had stolen the necklace for a girl. Many of the distasteful things I started doing were designed to get the attention of girls.

Before long, I began stealing on a regular basis. One day I stole eight or 10 boxes of Now & Later's and a half-dozen rolls of Sweet Tarts from the store down the street from our house. Unfortunately, a clerk in the store saw me and chased me out into the street. When I thought I had ditched him, I ran back to my house. But it turns out he was right behind me when I got to my front door. I went in thinking, "Please don't ring the doorbell." A few moments later, the doorbell rang. I tried to discourage my mom from answering it, but she insisted on opening the door. So I ran upstairs, locked myself in the bathroom, and started running the water, as if I were taking a shower.

A few minutes later, my mom came bounding up the stairs and started pounding on the locked door. "Donnie! Did you steal candy from the store?" she demanded to know. Mom made me go downstairs and give all the candy back and apologize to the man. Initially, I didn't want this man to ring the doorbell. Now I didn't want him to leave. As soon as he left, my mom gave me a whipping I'll never forget. That was the first time I got caught for stealing, but it wouldn't be the last.

Not long after her second divorce, my mom began dating again. One day she introduced me to a military officer, one who had the same first name I did, Donald. He wore a crisp, bright-white uniform and came across as being impressive and official. Ironically, my first impression of him wasn't the greatest. Officer Calloway was nothing like the men I was used to. He didn't have a foul mouth, wasn't shabbily dressed, and wasn't immature or lazy. In fact, he was the opposite of all those things. He acted differently than other men, and it was evident that my mother liked being around him. Yet I thought my mother was making a big mistake spending time with this individual.

I was still 10 years old when my Mom married Officer Calloway. I vividly remember the wedding, which was performed by a justice of the peace. It was the first time I had ever worn a suit. Although just 10 years of age, I was already jaded about marriage. At the wedding, I remember thinking to myself, "I wonder how long *this* marriage will last? I wonder what is going to happen to *this* guy?"

Soon after they married, my parents bought a house, and we moved as a family to Virginia Beach, the next big city over from Norfolk. My mom left the Navy when she got pregnant. Within a year, my parents had a son — my brother, Matthew. Matthew was the cutest little baby, and I loved holding him and playing with him.

Matthew's arrival also opened the door for me to more freedom because my parents were so preoccupied with a newborn. I expanded my horizons and met new friends in Virginia Beach. Like most kids my age, I started to get into all the popular things of the time, especially movies like *E. T.* and *Star Wars: Return of the Jedi.*

I was also into riding my bike, skateboarding, and hanging out at the beach. This is where my lifelong fascination with surfing began. All of these activities allowed me to go fast. It also helped me to get away from my parents. For example, there were big sand hills in the woods near my house, and I would go bike riding there with my friends. My mom asked me to keep within shouting distance, but I was always testing her to see what I could get away with. I remember thinking to myself, "You shouldn't be riding in these woods." But there was something exhilarating about crossing the line and seeing how far I could push things. And I soon found myself testing those boundaries more and more.

Around the time I turned 11 years old, I found myself beginning to get really attracted to girls — no doubt because of all the television I was watching. Almost every show I watched seemed to be enticing or seductive, at least for a pre-teen boy. *Three's Company* was all sexual innuendo. Girls in bikinis would come out between rounds on WWF Wrestling. On *Hee Haw,* you'd see a guy with missing teeth playing the banjo, a busty blonde sitting there beside him. I watched *Wheel of Fortune* to see Vanna White. I watched *The Price is Right* not so much to watch the models show the merchandise but to look at *their* merchandise. I even had a thing for Mallory (Justine Bateman) on *Family Ties,* a show whose underlying message, ironically enough, was to promote family values. Needless to say, I was very impressionable. Whatever I saw, it was never enough. I always wanted more.

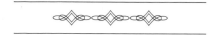

The other thing that my new father brought into my life — other than Matthew — was Christianity. My stepfather was Episcopalian. It was at this time that I was baptized at St. Peter's Episcopal Church in Norfolk, Virginia. While it was done in the name of the Father, the Son, and the Holy Spirit and I became a child of God, the baptism certainly didn't change our way of life. It was a cultural formality that we just did to get it out of the way.

In fact, I have no memory of the ceremony that took place inside the church. The only thing I remember is stepping outside afterwards and stuffing my face with jelly-filled donuts, the kind with the sugar frosting on the outside. That was my introduction to Christianity. It had nothing to do with a relationship with a loving God. I received a piece of paper and a plaque, which my parents filed away in a drawer. Then we went on with our essentially non-Christian lives.

Considering my upbringing, I guess it's no surprise that I didn't believe in God. For me, God was the equivalent of the tooth fairy or the Easter Bunny, a myth that so-called Christians made up in order to make children happy. It gave parents an excuse to give their kids gifts once or twice a year and get a day off of work. People winked and nodded and went along with the charade, but after the holidays were over, people went on with their real lives. I was convinced that nobody really believed in God.

4

GOING TO
CALIFORNIA

AS IT TURNED OUT, OUR NEW FAMILY wasn't long for Virginia Beach. One day, Dad came home from work and announced we would be moving west — all the way to San Pedro, California, a coastal town on the border of Orange and Los Angeles counties. The announcement was something of a surprise to me, since our family seemed to be putting down roots in Virginia Beach.

For one thing, my parents had bought a house in Virginia Beach and were busy spending time and money fixing up the place. My mom also seemed to be settling in and enjoying life as a stay-at-home mother. She had been discharged from the Navy while pregnant with Matthew, and with her new husband comfortably supporting the family, she finally had time to socialize. Most days she would take Matthew down to the local park in his stroller, no doubt showing him off to the other young mothers in the neighborhood. But in the end, my parents decided that my dad's latest career opportunity was simply too good to pass up.

Of course, being 10 years old I had no say in the move, but that didn't stop me from letting my parents know how upset I was about leaving Virginia Beach. I whined about how I'd have to leave all my friends. I whined about how I'd have to start all over again at a new school. But secretly I was most upset about leaving that cute girl I had recently developed a crush on.

Yet as soon as parents and friends began educating me about the joys of southern California, I stopped my complaining. In fact, the more I heard about California, the more excited I became about moving. Sure, Virginia Beach was nice. The girls were pretty, and I could go to the beach all the time. But that might be even more true in southern California.

And this being the early 1980s, California sounded like the place to be. Almost everything I was watching on television came from Hollywood. Most of the music I was listening to came from either Los Angeles or San Francisco. If everything I heard was true, I would soon be living right in the middle of where everything that was cool was happening. I might not have believed in heaven or hell, but southern California sure sounded like paradise to me.

In order to get to paradise, though, we had to make a very long trip in a very small car. We set out in the family car — a Toyota Corolla. Now this is the kind of car that's adequate for doing around-town errands, but it's not at all suited for transporting two adults, a child, and an infant cross-country. Today, a family would make the same trip in a big SUV, complete with a television and DVD player keeping the kids occupied all the while.

By comparison, I had it rough. There was no television in the Calloways' Corolla. I was scrunched in the back, sharing the space with Matthew's car seat and a couple of big duffel bags. The only entertainment I had was my own imagination.

The worst part, though, is that we made the trip in mid-summer and the Corolla didn't have air conditioning. Whenever the temperature went above 85 degrees — more often than not in the southern U.S. — it would get pretty uncomfortable. Driving straight through, we could have covered the 2,700 miles from Virginia Beach to Los Angeles in four or five days. But my parents decided to take the opportunity to sightsee and visit family. With dozens of scheduled stops, it took us more than three weeks to reach our final destination.

The first detours we took were close to home, visiting Mom's relatives in West Virginia and Dad's family in Asheville, North Carolina. My parents wanted to see as many relatives as possible, knowing that it might be some time before we might return to the East Coast.

After that, we hit the traditional tourist spots in Nashville and Memphis — before cutting through Arkansas, Oklahoma, and Texas on Interstate 40. Arkansas, for one, wasn't what I expected. I didn't picture it being so woody and mountainous. I had seen the movie *Deliverance* and that had colored the way my young mind imagined Arkansas. Oklahoma and Texas seemed fascinating, and I was amazed every time we passed one of those big commercial cattle ranches. There would be thousands of cattle grazing, the herd stretching as far as the eye could see. I had never seen so many animals all in one place. And I had never seen anything like the Wild West. For me, it was the most interesting part of the trip.

In New Mexico, we came across huge buttes and giant rock outcroppings, the kind of scenery I had only seen in movies. I was amazed at how one could see from horizon to horizon, something that wasn't possible back East with all the trees, lights, and buildings.

When I finally saw the Grand Canyon, I was mesmerized. I felt a mixture of awe and fear when I first got the chance to take it in. It was frightening to walk right up to the edge and peer down into the canyon. I found it especially strange to see a helicopter flying *below* me.

However, by the time we reached the Grand Canyon, I was ready to be there already —even if I didn't exactly know where *there was*. When we drove through the desert in Arizona, it was brutally hot, hotter than any temperatures I had ever experienced before. Of course, our old Corolla wasn't equipped with the exterior temperature display that's standard on virtually every car today, but I'll bet it was at least 110 degrees during the day. I remember my mother was constantly putting a wet towel on Matthew's forehead in an effort to keep him cool. Even the windows of the car were hot to the touch.

Before continuing on to California, we took a quick detour to Las Vegas, where my parents did some gambling. Meanwhile, I took in all that Circus Circus had to offer a kid. For me, the entire trip was a revelation. But Las Vegas — with all its neon lights —was especially captivating. I suddenly realized there was this whole dazzling world out there, and I was now getting to experience some of it. After Vegas, we took one last detour, passing through Death Valley National Park before taking the I-15 over to Los Angeles. My parents chose to cruise into town on the 101 Freeway, so that we could drive through Hollywood. From Hollywood Boulevard, we saw the famous Hollywood sign, the Capitol Records building, Grauman's Chinese Theatre, and the Sunset Strip. I could not believe we were going to be living in southern California, the center of where everything was happening.

We settled in the suburban community of San Pedro — just a few miles from the Pacific Ocean, so close that you could smell the sea in the air. Although we lived in military housing and all of our neighbors were military families, our neighborhood had the feel of a typical beach community — small, low-slung, one-story houses situated close together. The only thing that made the area atypical is that the neighborhood moms were an especially close-knit group, perhaps on account of how often their husbands were out at sea on patrol. Like most of the dads in the area, mine spent much of his time out in the Pacific, usually aboard a fast frigate named the *U.S.S. McClusky*.

As for me, my first introduction to California was everything I expected it to be and more. On my first day at school, I was fascinated by how *cool* the kids were. The guys had bleached blond hair and wore loose, baggy clothes with Vans or Converse sneakers. A lot of them had big, long earrings and were into skateboarding, which was just beginning to become popular courtesy of skater videos and the rising skateboard star Tony Hawk. But the most interesting thing about everyone is that they had their own way of talking and acting. It was the heyday of the Valley Girl, and even though San Pedro wasn't actually in the San Fernando Valley, it sure seemed like it. Oh, and surfing was very big there, too.

In the beginning, I was intimidated by my new environment. There were more people, more smog, and more traffic than I had ever seen before. On the roads, it seemed like rush hour was never-ending. And my school was bigger than any school in West Virginia or Virginia Beach. The class sizes weren't just huge, they were gargantuan. It wasn't uncommon for me to have 60 or 70 students in one of my core classes. And since everyone was just one among many, it wasn't easy to stand out. Perhaps that explains why so many students dressed and acted so outrageously.

In San Pedro, I also started getting exposed to different races for the first time. Sure, there were African-Americans in Virginia Beach, but there were more here. There were Filipinos, Japanese, Latinos, and Vietnamese. Many of the girls had naturally dark skin, and the ones that didn't seemed to be perpetually tan. People were different here, and I liked it. I wanted to soak in all of the culture and find a way to express myself, just like all the other cool kids were doing.

Naturally, I quickly started down the road to a very fast-paced lifestyle. I began listening to more music, usually popular heavy metal like Def Leppard, Scorpions, and Black Sabbath, but also synthesizer-driven bands like Depeche Mode, Tears For Fears, and Simple Minds. I started growing my hair long and started wearing a lot of band T-shirts. I vividly remember my mom getting upset the first time she saw me wearing an Ozzy Osbourne *Ultimate Sin* shirt. But what was she going to do?

Almost immediately, I started hanging out with the "wrong crowd." In my school, they were called the stoners. They were the guys with long hair who were into skateboarding and surfing. I liked them because they listened to the same music I did and because they always seemed to be hanging out with the prettiest girls. As far as I was concerned, those were both good things.

It wasn't long before my new friends introduced me to marijuana. I remember us sitting around one night and one of them casually asking if I'd ever tried pot? I hadn't, but I was definitely curious about what it was like. So I tried it. At the age of 11, I smoked a big, fat joint all by myself. Even back then, my approach was full-throttle. I wanted to make absolutely sure I got high, and I did.

In fact, I got so stoned that my sides started to hurt because I was laughing so hard. I got so confused that I didn't even know what was going on. I started eating everything in sight. Getting stoned opened up a whole new sensuous world to me. When my friends turned on the TV and I saw the girls on the screen — well, they just looked *delicious*. I wasn't just hungry for food, now I was hungry for everything.

Of course, when I got stoned, I would get cottonmouth and crave liquid refreshment. My new friends suggested alcohol. At first, I wasn't wild about the idea of drinking to quench my thirst. The first time I tried beer was back when I lived in Virginia Beach. My friends and I took a six-pack of cold Budweiser from one of my friends' dads. We ran into the woods with it, and because we weren't aware that Bud is best served ice cold, we let it get warm before we drank it. When I finally tasted the beer, I thought it was nasty. I remember thinking, "What's the big deal about drinking beer?" It didn't seem all that great to me.

I had similar first experiences with cigarettes and cigars. The first time I smoked a cigarette in Virginia Beach I didn't really like it. I coughed a lot, and it made my breath smell nasty. And the first time I tried a cigar — also swiped from a friend's dad — I inhaled and just about died. I didn't know that you weren't supposed to inhale cigar smoke.

But at the same time, I believed that there had to be something that made so many people want to smoke and drink. Maybe we didn't do it right in Virginia Beach, I thought, so eventually I broke down and decided to try beer again.

While I wasn't old enough to buy alcohol, my stoner friends had older brothers and sisters who would give it to us. We thought we were so cool — hanging out with the older kids, drinking beer, and listening to metal music. They would play their instruments for us, and their girlfriends would come over wearing tight jeans and leather jackets — the kind with all the tassels hanging down under the arms. To us, those girls were vixens — heavy metal goddesses.

During this time, I also began to do more with girls than just look at them. This opened up yet another world of possibilities for me. Girls made going to the beach a lot more interesting, too. Some of these California girls wore only the skimpiest bikinis. I could watch them all day long, especially if I was high. One time my friend, his dad, and I stumbled upon a nude beach in San Diego (Black's Beach). I had never seen anyone walk around naked before, but this was California, where anything was possible. And as it turns out, Black's Beach is one of the best surfing spots in all of SoCal.

Even though I was now beginning to exhibit bad behavior, I could still fool both my parents and strangers into thinking I was an innocent, all-American boy. I was far from innocent. Probably the worst thing I did while living in San Pedro was to start the California equivalent of a forest fire. In our neighbor-hood, there were eucalyptus trees — tall, light brown trees with leathery leaves that droop down from above. One day I was walking past one with my lighter in hand and just decided to stop and light it at the base. It was an impulse decision. It also turned out to be a big mistake.

I expected the wood to burn slowly, giving me plenty of time to put the fire out. But this tree didn't just go up in flames, it *exploded,* almost like a bomb had gone off. Flames began shooting off in all directions. Little did I know, but I had ignited a blue gum eucalyptus (the most flammable variety), which firemen sometimes refer to as "gasoline trees."

I panicked and started running away. In less than a minute, the surrounding field was on fire, a half-acre or more. A huge cloud of very dark smoke was bellowing up and begin-ning to envelop the entire area. I ran home to my house as fast as I could. When I burst in the door, I hurriedly said, "One of those guys just lit a fire!" My parents rushed to call the local fire department. Within minutes, fire trucks were on the scene, working feverishly to extinguish the blaze.

It took the firemen an hour to put the fire out. When they were done, the fire chief came over to our house to get more information about the arsonist. He asked, "What did this guy look like? Can you tell me what he was wearing? In which direction did he run?" Naturally, I gave him a fake description and sent him off in the wrong direction.

Afterwards, everyone was praising me as a hero for reporting the blaze and providing such a detailed description of the suspect. My parents were so proud. "That's my boy," my dad said.

Meanwhile, I had come kissing close to burning down all the houses in our neighborhood. Years later, when I told my parents what had really happened, they were speechless.

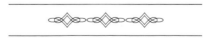

After living in San Pedro for about a year-and-a-half, my father came home one day and again told us he had just been assigned to a new duty station, so we would be moving yet again. We wouldn't be going far, just down the coast to a town called Santee in San Diego. I had been hearing a lot about San Diego from my friends. Everyone said it was *the* place to be and one of the best places to live, even better than San Pedro. After all, Black's Beach was there, and tons of other great places to surf and look at girls.

It turns out that San Diego was as good as advertised. In my opinion, the beaches were better and the girls were as good looking there as anywhere. But one big difference is that in Santee we weren't living in military housing. We lived in an apartment, right alongside the rest of your average folks.

This new environment allowed me to get out and have new experiences outside the military for a change. What I discovered is that the parents of my new friends were loose, at least as compared to other military moms and dads. My parents might not have been religious at that time, but they still kept a good house and were respectable people. They set down rules I was supposed to adhere to and established a curfew.

But a lot of my friends in San Diego came from broken homes. They lived with only one parent, and that parent invariably had to work during the day. So we could skip school, stay home, get stoned, and watch MTV while they were at work. If it was a weekend, my parents might call over and ask, "Is it okay if Donnie stays at your house for the day?" The parent would say yes, but then he'd end up going out drinking, so we'd be left in the house to do whatever we wanted. Or we would get dropped off at a beach somewhere and practice our surfing for hours.

Basically, close parental supervision was the exception in San Diego, not the rule. And when I think back on it now, I realize that some of my friends' parents were remarkably dysfunctional. For instance, I had one friend whose dad was into heavy metal and practically worshipped Ronnie James Dio, the diminutive rock singer who fronted Elf, Rainbow, and Black Sabbath before launching a solo career that continues to this day. Some people know him as the rocker who supposedly gave rise to the so-called heavy metal salute, with index and pinkie finger upraised.

Now, if you've heard any of Dio's good-versus-evil songs, you know that many of them have Dungeons & Dragons-type themes. Well, this man — this *parent* — decorated the interior of his home to look like a dungeon. The house was black, the curtains were black, even the furniture was black. There were candles burning everywhere and big swords hanging on the walls. When I first went over there, it spooked me, but then I thought, "Wow, there must be a big secret here."

Fittingly, the woman of the house looked like Lily from *The Munsters*. She had long black hair, dressed all in black, and wore black eyeliner. I found her scary but attractive and alluring at the same time. She fit right in with the ambience. This atmosphere was nothing like my house, which was bright and flowery, the windows always open to let in the breeze. In my mind, this place was nothing but spooky.

In contrast, I had another friend who was completely spoiled rotten. His parents were divorced, and he lived with his mom in a house that must have cost a million dollars. It had music piped in through the entire house, a huge fountain in the backyard, and a lawn so perfect it looked like a fairway at an exclusive country club. My friend got just about whatever he wanted. We would be flipping through magazines and he would yell out, "Mom, I want this ColecoVision." She was like, "Fine." And one week later, he'd have it. His mom treated us like royalty, too. She would order us pizzas and soda and bring us cookies upon request.

In contrast, nobody ever came to my house to hang out. I didn't want them to. If they did, we'd have to sit and watch an old Western with my parents or do whatever my parents were doing. It was a lot more fun for me to go elsewhere, where we could smoke weed and turn the music up really, really loud.

In Santee, I increasingly found myself living a double life. Around my parents, I was often a little darling, a cute kid who was still somewhat willing to obey the rules. But when I was with my friends, it was another story altogether. I started finding trouble at a popular hangout spot called "The Pit," a huge sand dune where my friends liked to go after school or on weekends.

Mainly, we would go there to get drunk and stoned and look at pornography. People would stash *Penthouse* and *Hustler* magazines in the brush there. We would find them and then spend hours looking at the pictures.

But sometimes we would go to The Pit with our bb guns and start shooting at birds. One time, we even brought an actual gun. One of my friends' dads was a border patrol guard and kept a loaded pistol in his house. We found it in a shoebox in the top of his dad's closet, then took it out to The Pit and fired off an entire clip. Of course, my parents knew nothing about this sort of behavior.

But even though I was doing a pretty good job of hiding most of my indiscretions, it was slowly becoming more obvious that I was becoming increasingly rebellious. Naturally, my parents didn't approve of the direction in which I was headed. They attempted to keep me on the straight and narrow, but to no avail. It was always, "You've got to do this, You've got to do that. You've got to be home by nine o'clock." Or, "Why aren't you going to school?" But I didn't like authority and eventually began to rebel against their rules and regulations. I started accusing them of watching over me all the time and oppressing me.

Around this time, I started to talk back to my parents. One time I saw one of those Columbia House ads that offered seven albums for a penny. Figuring it was a steal, I sent in a penny, Three weeks later, seven cassettes came in the mail — *Men At Work, Huey Lewis and the News,* whatever — along with a bill that came to a lot more than a penny. My parents were upset about the bill, saying, "I can't believe you did this without asking us. Now we have to either pay or send the cassettes back." My response? "Deal with it. Make it go away." They were shocked at my belligerence and said, "What? What's wrong with you?"

What was wrong with me was that by that time I just wanted to lie around and get stoned. Marijuana makes you really lazy. I totally lost interest in doing household chores, much less spending time with my parents. A whole day at a pottery factory with my mom? That was torture. I just wanted to be left alone to do my own thing.

It was probably inevitable, but eventually I played the "you're not my real dad" card with my stepfather. He got really mad at me over something and I said, "You can't tell me what to do! You're not my father!" I know that hurt him. I had never said anything like that to him up to that point.

After that, I started becoming very secretive. I began hiding my bad behavior and honed my ability to deceive and manipulate my parents. At the same time, I found myself slowly becoming more and more emotionally distanced. I found myself getting detached from the mother I once loved so much. And the more drugs I did and the more I drank, the more detached I became.

Still, I wasn't totally incorrigible — at least not yet. One day, I showed up at school for my first period math class, having skipped the previous day's class to get stoned with my friends. When I arrived, I found out there was a big test, which I was totally unprepared for. I stayed and took the test, but I copied all of my answers from the student sitting next to me.

When we got our grades back, I found out that I had aced the test. I should have been overjoyed at getting one over on the system. But this particular teacher, Mr. Apple — has there ever been a more apropos name for a teacher? — was so nice and so *authentic* that I started feeling guilty about what I had done.

The next day, I went up to him after school and admitted I had cheated on the test. I was shaking like a leaf when I approached him, thinking I was going to get totally busted. His response blew me away. He said, "I am going to drop your grade to a B, but I want you to know that it took a lot for you to admit that you cheated. I respect that. What you did was the right thing to do." I walked away thinking, "That's a cool dude." I guess I felt like his niceness required me to be honest with him. It would be one of the few times I felt guilty — let alone honest — about my actions or behavior.

After we had lived in San Diego for some time, my dad came home and announced it was time to move again. I wondered where on earth we could possibly be going. Malibu? Maui? So far, every place we moved had been better than the last. How great was the next place going to be? What would the waves and the girls be like there?

I had come to build my life around southern California. As far as I was concerned, I would have been happy to live there for the rest of my life. When my father said we'd be moving to a "far-away place," I braced myself for a shock — something I was not prepared to hear.

5

ORIENT
EXPRESS

IWENT STRAIGHT INTO SHOCK when my father announced we were moving to Japan. It felt as if my life suddenly came to an end. I had watched a lot of Saturday morning TV, and if the dubbed-in-English martial arts movies were any indication, Japan was about the last place I or any teenaged boy would want to live.

My mind raced as I imagined my life there. Would I spend all my time running from Kung-Fu masters out to kick my butt? Would I face the fire-breathing wrath of Godzilla? Would anyone even speak English? All I knew about Japan were the most wrong-headed stereotypes. I expected I would have to learn Japanese, dye my hair jet black, and eat raw fish every day.

And what about music, drinking, and drugs? What about girls on the beach and surfing? I imagined that all of that would have to come to an abrupt end, too. As far as I could tell, everything I had come to love in life would suddenly be taken away. Even more troubling was that the girls in those Japanese movies didn't look all that attractive to me. I thought I might never see a pretty blonde again.

Naturally, it wasn't long before I freaked out on my parents and declared, "I am not moving to Japan. I'm not going." I desperately looked for a way out. "How about I move back to West Virginia or North Carolina and live with Grandpa or Dad's family?" I really didn't want to move back with my hillbilly relatives, but living in the woods seemed preferable to spending the rest of my foreseeable future in Japan.

Here I was, just barely a teenager, trying to dictate to my parents where I was willing and not willing to live. They said, "Living with one of your relatives is *not* an option." Of course, they were right. What choice did I have?

Once I resigned myself to the fact that I had to move to Japan, I made an agreement with myself that when I got there I was going to openly rebel against my parents and any other authority figures who tried to keep me from having fun. My attitude was, "If you take me to Japan, you watch what happens. You think I'm bad now? Wait until you see what I'm like after you take me out of the paradise of southern California."

I didn't tell anyone about the pact I made with myself, but I was committed to following it through. And I was determined to become my parents' worst nightmare.

By this time in my life, I had moved on so many different occasions that I was accustomed to the packing and the transition of settling into a new home. But during this transition, I was in total denial about what was happening. I felt like — or at least held out hope — that this time it was all a big joke. My fantasy was that our family would get on a 747, and we would fly out over the Pacific. Then we'd make a big swooping turn and come right back home. No matter what I told myself I simply couldn't accept the fact that I was being forced to move to a foreign country — a place where I was expected to live for a minimum of three years.

When we departed on Japan Air Lines from Los Angeles International Airport, I was still in denial. During the 12-hour non-stop flight, the longest plane ride I had ever been on, I remember thinking to myself, "This cannot be happening to me. Please tell me that we are going to turn around and land at Universal Studios." I imagined deplaning, only to find a fake set of Japan — neon signs, fish markets, and a lot of small people riding around on bicycles. Yep, I was doing some serious wishful thinking.

The reality of my situation didn't hit home until I got off the airplane and was greeted by a line of Japanese men and women, who bowed their heads and gave us the traditional greeting for "Good morning." At that point, I knew I was in trouble. This was really happening. I was actually in Japan.

"So be it," I thought. "My rebellion begins right now."

But before I could actually start my plan, I had to get my feet on the ground, so to speak. That very first day we moved into our new home — a Quonset or prefabricated shelter made of corrugated iron that looks like a big tube. The fact that I didn't have a lot of privacy made the experience even less tolerable. Luckily, the arrangement was only temporary.

We lived there for a month until moving into proper officer's housing at my dad's assigned post, Atsugi Naval Air Facility.

With a name like Atsugi Naval Air Facility, one might assume the base is on the coast of Japan. I know I did. But even though Atsugi is technically a naval station, it's several hours' distance from the nearest seaport, and I didn't like that at all. Located on the Kanto Plain on the island of Honshu, Atsugi is just 20 miles from downtown Tokyo. It's within an hour's drive of other key U.S. military bases in Japan: namely, Camp Zama, Camp Fuji, and Yokota Air Base, which serves as a hub for American military flights in the Western Pacific.

The base's most distinguishing feature is its two huge airfields. Both of which have runways large enough to accommodate C-130s, those mammoth cargo planes that can comfortably transport tanks. Aircraft maintenance and testing facilities are also prominent on the base. In fact, if you go by appearance alone, one would expect Atsugi to be an Air Force facility. They even train Marines at Atsugi, making it quite cosmopolitan for a modern military operation.

As for its history, the U.S. military's association with Atsugi stretches almost all the way back to World War II. Originally constructed by the Japanese Imperial Navy in 1938, it was designed to serve as Emperor Hirohito's Kamikaze Naval Air Base. But after the Japanese unconditionally surrendered to the United States in 1945, it fell into disrepair before the U.S. Navy restored it and officially commissioned it a U.S. base in December 1950.

For the last 60 years, Atsugi has housed American sailors and their families, although it looks quite a bit different today than it did in the 1950s. Today, it has all the conveniences and amenities of a small town. There's a commissary, post office, video store, movie theater, bowling alley, gas station, swimming pool, gymnasiums, and both football and softball fields, not to mention an 18-hole golf course and a diverse array of restaurants that serve American and Japanese food. Atsugi is so immense that it takes almost three hours to walk from the front gate to the back gate. In fact, eight to 10 thousand American personnel live on the 1,249-acre facility at any one time, making it the Navy's largest base in the Pacific.

One of the few notable drawbacks to Atsugi is the abysmal air quality that handicaps the region. Although the climate is moderate — not unlike Norfolk or Virginia Beach; hot and humid in the summer but cold and occasionally snowy in winter — the pollen counts and pollution make Atsugi a nightmare for asthma and allergy sufferers. While the air isn't nearly as bad as it is in major cities like Tokyo and Yokohama, it's still an issue, especially nowadays.

Twenty years ago, all my family had to worry about was getting the proper vaccinations before leaving for Japan. I vividly remember the typhoid inoculation, which paralyzed my arm for a couple of hours. But today, the Navy takes a prospective candidate's medical conditions — and those of his family members — into consideration before assigning him to Atsugi. Such are the concerns about air pollution.

Although Atsugi is much like a city unto itself, it lacks one key feature found in just about every American town — a secondary school. All U.S. military dependents attend junior high or high school at Camp Zama, the headquarters of U.S. Army Japan, located 25 miles southwest of Tokyo and a little more than five miles from Atsugi. While five miles doesn't sound like much, the area's traffic and countless active railroad crossings makes for a long 45-minute commute. I would spend an hour-and-a-half on the bus each and every school day, an excruciating amount of time for a restless teenager.

To make matters worse, the bus we rode made your typical yellow American school bus look like a luxury vehicle. We were relegated to an old military bus with raggedy, uncomfortable seats. Mostly, I passed the time by listening to Iron Maiden on my Walkman — one of those super-slim models not much larger than a cassette tape — or talking with friends about what I did the night before. If I didn't do my homework, I would take the opportunity to copy it from one of my classmates.

On my first day of school, I simply wasn't mentally prepared to deal with meeting my new classmates. I was expected at school less than 24 hours after touching down in Tokyo, so I had no time to get adjusted to my new surroundings. Of course, I was also jetlagged and still somewhat bewildered about everything that was happening. My parents dropped me off at the assigned bus stop. But when the bus arrived, I didn't get on. I just couldn't. I let the bus drive away without me, figuring I could bum around all day and no one would be any wiser. Unfortunately, the principal called my parents when I didn't show up in homeroom, and they got extremely upset when they found out I had cut school on the first day.

"Why didn't you go to school?" they asked. I lied and told them I missed the bus. Although I wanted to tell them I intentionally cut school, I still was a bit hesitant about acting out against my parents so soon. I needed time to get my bearings in this strange land before I would feel totally comfortable about rebelling. At the same time, I was pragmatic. I was conscious of the fact that if I wanted to start making new friends, I had to start going to school. After all, the military school was one of the few places I could go where everyone spoke English. And that was where the girls were, too.

When I did make it to school the next day, I was surprised to find that many of the students — maybe even the majority — were half-Japanese. Typically, the students' mothers were Japanese and their fathers were either sailors or officers in the American military. Those kids had a very interesting look, a hybrid of features — American and Japanese — that made them look both unique and very appealing.

In the course of moving from West Virginia to Norfolk to Virginia Beach to Los Angeles to San Diego, I had attended five different schools in just six years. Experience taught me that I had no choice but to be outgoing, because that was the only way I had a chance to make new friends. They certainly weren't going to come to me because I was always on the move.

At first, I was intimidated by my new classmates, so I looked to strike up conversations with all-American boys with whom I might have something in common. I started introducing myself to the kids who wore the black concert T-shirts, as music was something I knew we could bond over. If a guy had long hair and wore a Led Zeppelin or Ozzy Osbourne T-shirt, I knew it was probably someone I'd be comfortable hanging out with.

As it turns out, I had no reason to feel intimidated. When I told my new classmates I had just come from southern California, they were immediately impressed. Many of them had been in Japan for years and wanted to know all about the latest U.S. music and happenings. From a technology perspective, Japan was clearly cutting-edge, but it could not compare to American pop culture. Being the definitive source of the latest and greatest information about music and culture certainly helped me to connect with the kids at school.

It also helped that I was into partying, as my new friends were definitely on the rebellious side and always up for having a good time. As the days progressed, I found myself drinking more and more, partially for the purpose of conforming and partially as a means of escape. In the beginning, I hated living in Japan so much that I got wasted just to forget about my predicament. Soon I was drinking to fit in.

Luckily for me, alcohol is much easier for a teenager to get in Japan than it is in the United States. For instance, if you go to a Wal-Mart or supermarket in the U.S., there's always a row of vending machines outside where one can buy bottled water, sports drinks, and soft drinks. In Japan, those same machines are stocked with all sorts of alcoholic beverages. As long as you are tall enough to put your Yen in the machine, you can access the beer or hard liquor of your choice — any time, day or night. As a result, I had virtually 24/7 access to booze. My drink of choice was Japanese vodka, mostly because it was clear and came in a cool-looking bottle. But rum, whiskey, and even rice wine would do the trick if vodka wasn't available.

As is the case with many teenagers, all the alcohol that I drank led me down a slippery slope to experimenting with hard drugs. Before long, I was snorting heroin and cocaine, all of which seemed to be easily accessible, even to someone only 13 years old and in junior high school. However, I didn't even want to be *near* anyone who was using needles to get high, not necessarily because I feared blood-borne diseases, but because I associated needles with pain. I was as pain-averse as anyone.

As a result, I only used opium when I could get it in a form where it could be sprinkled on a joint.

More frequently, though, I would end up doing either cocaine or heroin. Heroin made me feel extremely mellow. When I was high on heroin, someone could punch me and I'd be oblivious to the pain. On the other hand, cocaine gave me the opposite feeling. I would get this rush of energy and feel the blood flowing through my veins. The problem I had with cocaine is that the high never lasted that long — maybe 30 or 45 minutes. Then I would want more — immediately.

With the exception of avoiding needles, I wasn't particularly discriminating when it came to my choice of drugs. I was willing to do anything to get high. I began drinking cough syrup because it had codeine in it. I started sniffing gasoline and huffing (sniffing lighter fluid) because I could get high from the butane. I even went so far as to research which over-the-counter medicines contained ingredients that might get me high. Then I would take absurdly large doses to see if I could get a buzz. If it might possibly get me high, my attitude was, "Bring it on!"

I just couldn't help but take things to the extreme. Among all my friends, I was always the one to finish off the rest of the vodka, not to mention each and every half-empty beer. I would burn my lips trying to get everything out of a joint. I would even scrape the resin out of the bowl of a water bong just to get that little bit extra.

I was relieved when we finally got out of the Quonset hut and into our permanent residence — a second-floor apartment in the officer's housing compound at Atsugi. Even though we had above-average accommodations owing to my dad's officer status, the apartment still wasn't the greatest place to live. It wasn't in an ideal location either. The apartment overlooked the teen center, where I hung out a lot. It was also across the street from the day care center, so the area was always on the noisy side. With new people moving in every two or three years, housing on foreign military installations tends to take a beating, and to put it kindly, our apartment looked well-worn.

On the other hand, I had a nice view of Mount Fuji — Japan's tallest and most famous mountain — from my bedroom window. Every year about 200,000 people hike to the top of its 3,776-meter summit, making it perhaps the most frequently climbed peak in the world. Ironically, it's known as the "Purple Mountain," even though it's a volcano and snow-capped for most of the year.

Overall, my parents seemed pretty pleased with our living arrangements. From my dad's perspective, being stationed in Japan was certainly preferable than some of the alternatives. It was better than being somewhere like Libya, or some other country where the people were openly hostile to the United States. Today, North Korea is considered an especially dangerous rogue nation, but at the time, the Far East was pretty far away from the world's hot spots.

However, the fact that we were on a military base in a foreign country may have given my parents a false sense of security in regards to how much trouble I could get into. While there were often Japanese protesters outside the gates — usually protesting the behavior of American servicemen or the noise pollution from the endless parade of cargo and fighter planes — it was a guarded, gated community. So one could easily get complacent about safety and exposure to negative influences.

Personally, I never felt totally comfortable being there. Between the protesters and the barbed wire fence, you were always aware of being on foreign territory and that you weren't necessarily wanted. Most of the time you didn't experience any overt hostility, although on one occasion someone launched a shoulder-fired missile onto the base. It was the kind of incident that made you think twice about what was happening outside the gates.

Initially, my parents may also have wrongly assumed I wouldn't have access to drugs and alcohol in such a controlled environment. After all, there was no way a 14-year-old could buy alcohol on a military base. So when I was inside the gates, there was nothing to worry about, right?

The problem was that there were plenty of 21- and 22-year-old sailors at Atsugi, and they weren't exactly a positive influence on me. I wasn't supposed to go visit their barracks. But, of course, I would, just to party and listen to their stories.

And these guys partied hard, too. They had fridges filled with booze and usually started drinking in the barracks before heading out into the Japanese community to pick up girls. Sometimes they would end up getting into bar fights, swinging pool cues and chairs indiscriminately.

On the one hand, I saw these enlisted men as cool guys, in part because they were able to get me booze. But at the same time, I pitied them because they had to abide by all the Navy's stupid rules. They lived in gray, institutional-looking barracks and had to follow orders — people always telling them to shave or iron their clothes or polish their shoes. These sailors would always tell me how much being in the Navy sucked — that they were only going to do it for three years and then they were out. They looked forward to getting back to the States, growing their hair long again, surfing their home-break, and maybe even starting a band.

When they would get drunk, they would tell me — in graphic detail — about their encounters with Japanese girls. Then, in the same sentence, they'd tell me about the gonorrhea and syphilis and other diseases they caught. A lot of the stuff they told me I didn't even understand, but I sure was fascinated with their wild ways.

Meanwhile, I was also getting into plenty of trouble with kids my own age. Although the base had a youth curfew, I, of course, ignored it. Almost every night, I would sneak out of my second-floor window and slide down the pipes that ran up the side of my apartment building. On occasion, I would lose my grip and take a bad fall.

A few times, when I needed to be particularly discrete, I even jumped out of my bedroom window to the ground below. It's amazing that I never broke my ankle or suffered any other serious injuries. It's equally amazing that my parents never caught me on my way in or out.

Once out of the house, I would roam around the base with my friends, spray-painting buildings or hot-wiring golf carts at the golf course and then riding up and down the fairways. One of our favorite activities was spelunking or exploring caves. Before the Second World War, the Japanese constructed a labyrinth of caves under the present-day golf course, which they used for munitions storage and hiding. The entrances were tiny and hard to see — usually obscured by bamboo — but after you crawled through the tiny entrance hole, they would open up into vast caverns. The servicemen on the base warned us never to enter the caves because there was unexploded ordnance in there. But, of course, we ignored them.

Explosives aside, the caves were definitely scary if you were bold enough to go deep inside. After going in about 75 feet, you would look back and see *nothing* but a tiny spot of light from the entrance. If you went any further than that, you could see nothing. Of course, there were also a lot of bats, funky looking spiders, and who knows what else in there. Most of the time, we brought in flashlights to light the way, but sometimes we would use Bic lighters. Obviously, the unexploded bombs didn't scare us. One time, we found a couch in one of the caves. So the next time we brought in lighter fluid, we set it on fire.

Another favorite activity among us teens was shooting off our bb guns. Being around military personnel, weapons, and war machines, we soaked in the atmosphere and liked to pretend we were soldiers. Except in practice, we did more than pretend.

My friends and I would get modified KG9s and Uzis, automatic rifles that can hold 200 rounds. Then we would buy carbon dioxide packs that you can mount on your back, which thrust air pressure through the gun for more power. Highpowered, modified bb guns are commonplace in Japan, where ordinary citizens are not allowed to own guns that fire bullets. But the bb's sold in Japan are so large and the modifications make the guns so powerful that they may as well discharge real bullets. If you got hit in the temple with a bb fired from one of these guns, it would mean certain death.

But we were fearless. We would go into one of the wooded areas on the base and fire off 50 rounds at a time, mowing down bamboo trees in the process. Or we'd play war games, much like people play paintball today. Except we fired bb's at each other, and we never wore any eye protection, much less body armor. Even though we agreed never to fire at anyone's head, it's amazing that no one lost an eye. When we fought our pretend battles, I would end up with huge welts all over my body. One time Nathan shot me at point-blank range with his modified KG9. It left a purplish welt that was four inches wide and took a month to heal.

Although I was definitely the primary instigator of trouble among my friends, I got into plenty of trouble on my own, too. Looking back, the deterioration of my behavior roughly corresponded with the deterioration of my appearance. I started growing my hair long and began doing all manner of funky things with my hair.

Then, when I was about 14, I started dressing like I was from another planet. I would wear ripped jeans with holes in the knees along with a thin, black jacket that had lightning bolts on it. My girlfriends would refine my look by asking me to wear eyeliner or nail polish. Or they would insist on putting hairspray in my hair. Naturally, I wanted to please the girls I was hanging around with, so I went along with almost anything they wanted.

One night, a girlfriend convinced me to pierce one of my ears. I wanted to appease her, but I was such a wimp about not wanting to feel the pain that I slugged vodka while she held ice cubes to my ear — for an hour or so — to anesthetize the area. Then she punctured my ear lobe with an unsterilized needle. I left the needle in overnight, so a hole would form.

When she pulled the needle out the next morning, blood started flowing from the hole. We didn't know what to do. After the bleeding stopped, pus started to leak out. Before long, I had a raging infection. It just didn't look right. Between the pus and the scab that had formed, I was concerned my parents would notice what I had done.

At first, I tried to hide it, making sure to walk past them with my head turned so they wouldn't see. But eventually my mom noticed and freaked out. I'm not sure what she was more upset about — that I got my ear pierced or that the hole was so hideously infected. I told her, "There's nothing you can do about it now, so don't worry about it." When the infection finally cleared up, I started wearing a stud.

As my appearance changed, so did my taste in music, which was becoming an increasingly big part of my life. A lot of my friends were really into rock music and played instruments. That eventually inspired me to learn guitar. Heavy metal was all the rage in Japan, and a never-ending stream of British and American bands came to Tokyo, usually packing the 15,000-seat Budokan for multi-night engagements. At every opportunity, I went to see bands like Iron Maiden, Bon Jovi, Ratt, W.A.S.P., and Motley Crue. When there wasn't a good American or European band in town, I would go see Japanese heavy metal bands, many of which were very good, although I couldn't understand the words. A few of the Japanese bands — namely, Loudness — sang in English, but the lyrics were usually so silly that I just laughed when I heard them.

Of course, being a long-haired American boy with a pierced ear, ripped jeans, and makeup, I looked remarkably like many of the American heavy metal stars of the time, which made me extremely popular with young Japanese girls. Just by my being associated with the heavy metal scene, girls would be all over me. After a concert, my friends and I would lie and say that we were part of the road crew for Bon Jovi or Ratt or whoever. The girls would go crazy and just start screaming. I always felt like I was the man, like I was wanted. For me, going to heavy metal concerts was like going to heaven.

It didn't take long before even I realized that I was beginning to develop something of a superiority complex. It wasn't just the reaction I got from the girls. I was just physically bigger than most of the Japanese guys my age. I remember going into a shoe store to buy a pair of Converse sneakers. When the Japanese salesman measured my feet, he started to talk excitedly to the other clerks. He couldn't believe I had size 10 feet. Most of his customers were around size six, so, in comparison, I was a monster. I loved the attention and loved the feeling of dominating almost everyone around me.

Meanwhile, the relationships I was developing were just as dysfunctional as my appearance. On the military base, I met a half-Filipino girl — her mother was Filipino, while her father was in the military — who was really into punk rock. Initially we bonded over music. Together, we listened to bands like the Violent Femmes, Suicidal Tendencies, and the Dead Kennedy's. But before long, our relationship became very physical.

While she was a beautiful petite girl with dark skin and long, black hair, she wasn't exactly sane. To begin with, she had low self-esteem. Correction: she had *very* low self-esteem. She liked to be called "Dirt" — literally. And in a sick way, she kind of wanted me to treat her like it.

Still, no matter what abuse I inflicted on her, it was nothing compared to what she did to herself. In her mind, pain was cool, and she enjoyed self-mutilation. One time, we were hanging out together and she started toying with my double-edged butterfly knife, which I always kept razor sharp. She had no idea how sharp I kept the blade. Without warning, she made her lower leg really taut. Then, before I could get across the room to stop her, she used my knife to cut across the back of her ankle.

When I saw blood begin to gush out of the wound, I panicked. I ran to the nearest phone, which happened to be at the McDonald's on the base, and called my mom for help. By the time my mom drove her to the hospital, the whole back seat of my mom's car was covered in blood. The white towels we used to absorb the blood were soaked through and through. We carried her into the hospital, and her foot was just hanging there by what seemed like a thread.

In the Emergency Room, the doctors asked, "How in the world did this happen?" What was I going to say? I had to tell the truth. Luckily, the surgeons were able to repair the damage, but she had to go to physical therapy for weeks before she was fully healed. Had she cut just a little bit deeper, she would have never walked again.

As one might expect, incidents like this made my parents increasingly nervous. They tried to exert stronger control over my behavior in hopes of keeping me out of trouble. But that only made me want to rebel even more. As a result, my relationship with my parents became increasingly tenuous.

After a while, I simply stopped caring about hiding my dangerous and self-destructive behavior. When we first arrived in Japan, I would at least make the effort to put Visine in my eyes before coming home from a night of smoking marijuana. But eventually even that seemed too much of an inconvenience. Anyway, I was getting yelled at virtually every time I came through the front door, so what was the point of making an effort to hide my vices?

To avoid my parents, I started spending more and more time away from home. I would tell my mom or dad I was going to spend the night at a friend's house. But I would never go to that friend's house at all. Instead, I would run off to clubs and discotheques in Tokyo or Yokohama, sometimes even sleeping on the beach all weekend. Of course, my parents were furious when, for example, I would leave home on Friday morning and not return until late Sunday evening.

Meanwhile, I was getting into more and more run-ins with the police, both on and off the base. One time, the military police found me in possession of alcohol and threw me in the brig. They said they were going to contact my parents, but they never did. They did it just to scare me, although I'm not sure how much I would have cared if they did tell my parents.

Then one fateful day I walked into the PX — the exchange, a kind of general store on the base — wearing my black trench coat. I wanted to impress a girl, so I slipped a couple of stuffed animals and a handful of cassette tapes under my coat. Then I walked out the door, intending to take them directly to her house. The only problem is that someone in the store observed me and called the military police, who once again hauled me off to the brig. This time they didn't hesitate to call my dad, who was both embarrassed and angry that his son had been caught stealing on the base. It wouldn't be long before word of my antics would get around to his subordinates, making him look bad.

When my mom and dad came in to retrieve me from the lockup, I fabricated a story about how I knew what I did was wrong and how I kind of hoped I would get caught. I told them I missed the United States and hoped that a shoplifting charge would get me deported. "Will this get me sent back home?" I asked, as I started to get teary-eyed. "I miss the United States so much. I just want to go home."

It became a psychological game, and everyone started to almost feel sorry for me. So I played it for all it was worth. They told me, "No, unfortunately, you have to live here for a certain period of time. Your dad is stationed here, so you are just going to have to deal with it."

"Okay," I sniffled, "but you're not going to lock me up or make me go to counseling now are you?" Amazingly, they bought my whole manipulative routine and let me go with nothing more than a warning — a slap on the wrist.

Suckers. What they didn't know is that I didn't miss the United States anymore. In fact, I was starting to really love Japan. I started to think I might want to live the rest of my life there.

6

TOKYO NIGHTS

A T SOME POINT, IT MUST HAVE BECOME CLEAR to my parents that I was a thief. Initially, I did my best to hide the smoking, drinking, and drug use, but concealing thousands of dollars of stolen merchandise presented an even greater challenge. My bedroom — the only place I could stash what I stole — was quickly becoming filled with high-priced goodies lifted from stores all over the island of Honshu. Among other things, I amassed an impressive collection of guitars, amplifiers, stereos, surfboards, and skateboards. So my parents began to wonder where I was getting all this stuff. They were right to be suspicious. How many times could I lie and say that I was just borrowing from my friends?

Eventually, the sheer volume of "hot" items in my bedroom made it so patently obvious I was stealing that even I didn't bother to hide it anymore. For example, I would casually come home with two brand new electric guitars, defiantly walking through the front door with one in each hand. When my mom asked where I got them, I would mumble my now standard reply, "Leave me alone."

I would take the guitars to my room, slam the door, and blast heavy metal music — in effect, warning my mom and dad to keep their distance. It worked well.

After these confrontations, I'm sure my parents were thinking, "What do we do with Donnie? How do we deal with him?"

In hindsight, I know it must have been a stressful time for them, but what could they do? I was young, defiant, and rebellious. When my parents tried to enforce the rules they set down, I would simply ignore them. When they yelled at me or told me I was grounded, I wouldn't even respond. I would just curse and stomp out the front door. Talking to me was like talking to a brick wall.

Still, my parents tried to remain optimistic about the situation. As parents, I am sure they hoped I would grow out of it. They convinced themselves that I was just going through a phase, one that would pass in a year or two. They rationalized that I just needed a little more time to mature. We were clearly both in our own form of denial.

By the time I turned 15, living with my family became untenable. Every time I was in the same room with either my mom or dad, the air was thick with tension. My relationship with my parents deteriorated to the point where I couldn't have cared less about either of them. I had become so distant emotionally that I had no feelings for them whatsoever.

The only bond that I had left with my family was with my little brother, Matthew. When it came to him, I felt terribly, almost unexplainably conflicted. Ten years younger than I, he would often plead, "Brother, play with me." A part of me wanted to stay home and be the big brother I wanted to be and thought he needed. But I was so preoccupied with my girlfriends and drug buddies that I didn't want to commit to anything domestic.

Being rebellious seemed like the only thing I was willing and able to commit to, and I wanted to make sure that I followed through. So what if I occasionally felt pangs of guilt about abandoning Matthew. My solution? I didn't allow myself to think about him too much.

Today, almost 20 years later, it still pains me that I wasn't there for him when he was growing up and that he didn't have a big brother to look up to. There was a 10-year period when I was not a brother to him. I would give my life for him now, and in recent years, I've tried to make it up to Matthew. But all that lost time is still a wound.

Around the time that my relationship with my parents was crumbling, my social life unexpectedly came apart, too. During my first two years at Atsugi, I developed a close relationship with three guys who were my age. But like other military dependents, it meant they would leave Atsugi when their parents moved on to their next duty station. As it happened, all three friends went back to the U.S. at almost exactly the same time: one moved back to Florida, another to California, and the third to Washington state. One by one, I lost all my closest friends, and there was nothing I could do about it.

To make matters worse, my Filipino-American "girlfriend" also returned to the U.S. when a relative died. She returned to California for the funeral and an indeterminate period of mourning. Although her absence was only supposed to be temporary, her departure rattled me to the core. Most of my friends were already gone. Now my girlfriend had also gone away, and I didn't know when she would be coming back.

It was around this time that I began to pal around with Tommy. We had hung out together in the past, but we weren't really good friends. In many ways, he was a lot different than I. He was something of a loner; whereas, I had no problem being around a lot of people. But with all my friends gone, I was motivated to get to know him better. So we soon bonded over our mutual love for girls and music. We liked the same bands and talked about music night and day. Tommy wasn't the easiest guy to get to know, but after a while, we became close.

Once Tommy and I started hanging out, I realized that he could be a real asset to me. For one thing, he was smooth with the ladies. He taught me a lot about how to pick up girls. Also, he tended to be a little more cautious and restrained than I, particularly when it came to getting drunk. I had no inhibitions and would go all-out, but he knew when to stop. I got a measure of comfort knowing that at least one of us would be under control when we were out on the town. We were a good team.

But even though Tommy was cautious about most things, he could still be impetuous. We would be sitting around having an ice cream cone somewhere and suddenly he'd announce, "Dude, let's go here." Then we would just get up and go. There was never any conversation about the details of how we would get there or what we were going to do when we arrived. We would just go. I loved that feeling of spontaneity. It made hanging around with him fun and unpredictable. I had found my perfect partner-in-crime.

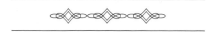

Having a rebellious spirit wasn't the only thing Tommy and I shared. Tommy had a terrible relationship with his family, just like I did. While wasted, we would often bash our parents. It became one of our favorite pastimes. We would moan about how sick we were of rules and how sick we were of getting yelled at.

It was during one of these complaining sessions that Tommy turned to me and — out of the blue — said, "Why don't we just run away? I know a girl's house in Tokyo we can stay at for a few days, and then we can go from there."

"Sounds good to me," I replied. On the spot, I agreed that we should run away. Immediately.

No thought was put into the decision at all. We had no concept of how or where we were going to live or what we were going to do for money. Not to mention how we would get by without speaking Japanese. It didn't concern us in the least. Shortly after that conversation, we simply walked off the base and into the Japanese community. We didn't even take any of our belongings from home, just the clothes on our backs.

For the first few days, we were elated at being out from under the control of our parents, who must have been worried sick when they realized we were gone. As expected, Tommy's girlfriend was more than happy to put us up for a few days, and we partied with her like there was no tomorrow. But after the initial euphoria of "being free" wore off, Tommy and I began to wonder what we were going to do for money. We discussed our options, and thievery seemed to be the most promising solution.

After all, we both had plenty of experience stealing consumer goods. In the past, we had often traded the merchandise for drugs, even though the so-called "exchange rate" was terrible. For instance, we would get two marijuana joints in exchange for a $200 guitar, which we were satisfied with. But that was when we were living at home and didn't necessarily need a lot of cash. Now that we were on our own we had different priorities, and having a steady supply of cash was at the top of the list.

Our first instinct was to steal women's purses, but we soon discovered that wasn't exactly the easiest or most lucrative way to gain money. For one thing, you usually had to rip the purse off the woman's arm. The victim would scream and make a fuss or maybe even get thrown to the ground in the ensuing struggle. If you were lucky, the strap would break and the purse would come free right away. But more often than not, witnesses would end up chasing us, which was another annoyance. And then, even when one of us got a purse, there might only be a small amount of cash inside. There had to be an easier way to generate income.

As it turned out, there was an easier way. As luck would have it, the girl we were staying with had a few contacts with a Japanese gang. Her contacts were young, but they were bona fide members and very intrigued about our interest in the gang. Being young and Caucasian really set us apart from everyone else involved with the group.

So as improbable as it sounds, we started hanging out with them a lot.

By mafia standards, everything we did was small-time stuff. The gang wasn't going to trust two easily recognizable Caucasian boys with smuggling opium or any other high-risk activity with which they were involved. Nevertheless, they gave Tommy and me the impression we might one day graduate to more substantial (and more lucrative) crimes and eventually have the opportunity to become full-fledged members.

While I certainly thought being involved with the gang was cool, I wasn't sure how I felt about becoming a member. In particular, I harbored concerns about the initiation rites, one of which involved getting the tip of your little pinkie cut off. Remember, I was a baby about getting my ear pierced. How could I possibly stand and watch a gang member hack off my pinkie with a meat cleaver?

In the meantime, it was hard to turn down the financial opportunities presented by the group. By our standards, the income we generated by working with them was great, and every "job" guaranteed an exciting adventure. But I had had my share of adventures even before becoming associated with a Japanese gang.

For example, another incident had occurred in a train station just before Tommy and I ran away from home. I had gone to Camp Zama with my friend Joel to crash a school dance. When we arrived, we immediately picked up two girls and got wasted with them. It wasn't until it came time to leave the dance that we realized we didn't have any means of taking the girls home.

So Joel — who was quite adept at stealing cars — suggested we go outside and steal a four-door sedan. That would solve our transportation problem. He picked out a car on the street and proceeded to hot-wire it. Then we drove it away, as casually as if the car belonged to us.

Joel was driving with his "date" in the front passenger seat, while I was in the back seat with the other girl. As we drove the girls back home, I noticed that Joel was having a hard time keeping the car from swerving back and forth. I was too high to complain, and since there weren't many cars on the road, I figured we would get home okay. Of course, being blind drunk, I didn't take into account that Joel might hit a stationery object.

I was just about to doze off in the back when suddenly my body was violently thrown forward into the seat in front of me. As it turns out, Joel had crashed head-on into a guardrail. Luckily, Joel and the girl next to me were unhurt, but the girl sitting in the front passenger seat had her head smack into the windshield. Hard. Naturally, she began panicking when she felt blood streaming down her face. Joel and I were so drunk and tired that we didn't want to be bothered with getting this girl medical care. We just wanted to get back home, so we could crash. Being the gentlemen that we were, we walked the girls to the nearest train station and sent them on their way.

Meanwhile, we still had to get home ourselves, so we looked for a train that would take us back in the direction of Atsugi. Neither of us relished the idea of taking public transportation. It would be a long ride back to the base, and we were both getting irritable. When we boarded the appointed train, we found ourselves in an empty rail car. I plunked myself down in one of the passenger seats, but Joel was so drunk that he couldn't even sit up. He was sitting hunched over on the floor when three Japanese guys — about our age but maybe a little older — got on at the next stop.

Almost immediately, one of them came over and asked Joel for a cigarette. It wasn't an idle request. It was patently obvious that Joel had "a pack rolled up in his T-shirt sleeve" — to borrow a phrase from a Jim Croce song. But Joel, who could speak a little bit of Japanese, defiantly replied that he didn't have one. And even if he did, he wouldn't be giving one to a Jap. At that point, I realized we were going to get into trouble. This Japanese kid pressed the issue. He pointed out that he could see a pack of Marlboro Lights under Joel's shirtsleeve. Joel's response? He started mocking the guy and cursing at him in Japanese.

I tried to get Joel to stop, but he was relentless. Meanwhile, the three Japanese guys huddled together and began conversing among themselves. I knew we were in trouble. There was no one to intervene or call for help if a fight broke out. I whispered to Joel, "We need to get off this train at the next stop." I knew we weren't going to get out of this without a confrontation, especially considering the fact that the five of us were the only passengers in the car and we were still four or five stations away from Atsugi.

At the next stop, I literally dragged a drunken Joel off the train. He could barely walk under his own power. Sure enough, the three Japanese guys got off, too. We were now alone on the platform. As soon as the train pulled away, one of the guys grabbed Joel from behind, spun him around, and punched him square in the face. Of course, I had to defend my friend. I turned around, and in my drunken stupor, sluggishly said, "Hey!" Then I started throwing punches.

The problem for both Joel and me was that they were three guys who were sober and quick. We were outnumbered in more ways than one. They started raining blows on us so fast that I didn't even know who was hitting me or where the punches were coming from. Within seconds, they knocked me onto the tracks. Luckily, a train wasn't entering the station or I could have been killed. But once I was down on the tracks, I realized I was better off staying there. I certainly didn't want to get back up and continue fighting on the platform. Nothing short of an incoming train was going to motivate me to get back up there.

Meanwhile, up above, the three guys were beating Joel senseless. Good friend that I was, I started running down the tracks to where the platform ended, where I could jump the fence and make my escape. As I was running away, I heard Joel tumble onto the tracks behind me. His body made a sickening thud on impact. He slowly got up and started stumbling after me, no doubt also hoping to escape in the same manner.

When Joel finally caught up to me at the end of the platform, we were both scared to death. I was hurting from the blows I had absorbed, but he was in much worse shape than I. He had blood pouring down his face and out of his mouth. It was clear we couldn't go back to Atsugi in the state we were in; people would ask questions.

Now wide awake from the adrenaline rush, we decided to take a detour to Joel's mother's house to see if she could bandage us up, saving a seemingly inevitable trip to the hospital. Both Joel's mom and dad were employed at Atsugi, but they divorced during their stay in Japan. So his mom had moved to an off-base community. When we showed up, it was late. She was a little drunk but sober enough to clean and bandage our wounds. Then she put us up for the night, so we wouldn't have to return to the base immediately.

After spending a little time with Joel's mom the next morning, I came to understand where Joel got his reckless bravado. He had inherited it from his mom. She was kind of crazy, and I was relieved when it was time to leave.

Concerning the gang, Tommy and I never had to worry about the possibility of getting fully initiated because we wore out our welcome. Our eventual undoing was the relationship we had with the gang's girlfriends. While the girls thought we were cute and amusing — almost like toys — some of their boyfriends got jealous when they saw that we were magnets for Japanese girls, especially the hottest ones. We loved all the attention, but these guys got extremely jealous. When we got drunk together, these feelings would come out in pushing and cursing sessions.

Luckily, the Japanese typically give their enemies a warning before getting violent. In America, these guys might have taken us somewhere and beaten us to a pulp. Instead, in typical Japanese fashion, they began to ignore us and lock us out of gang activities. This was fine by us. We began distancing ourselves from them and eventually fled to another city, confident that we could go out on our own and start our own little crime ring.

And that's exactly what we did. Our typical approach was to sleep by day and "work" at night. For the most part, we stayed in capsular hotels — institutional, block buildings where one can rent a space for a day or night. And when I say a "space," I mean that literally. You go inside to the front desk and plunk down the Japanese equivalent of six or seven dollars. What you get basically is a hole in the wall with nothing but a futon and coin-operated television inside.

In fact, the interior hallways of these capsular hotels bear a strong resemblance to cocoons or beehives. There are rows of niches cut into the wall on each side — usually stacked three high — into which you literally crawled.

Once inside, there was really only two options; either sleep or watch porn on the TV screen. All belongings were kept in a locker adjacent to your space. There simply wasn't room for anything inside your little cocoon. When we stayed in these places, I always felt like a larvae hatching. But it was the closest thing we had to call home, and I made the best of it.

The only feature of these capsular hotels that Tommy and I never got used to was the common bathrooms — and common baths. In other words, if you wanted to bathe, you had to walk down the hallway in your little towel and then get into a big pool of steaming hot water with a bunch of strange Japanese businessmen. A shower — much less a private shower — wasn't an option. Tommy and I just weren't into this pseudo-sauna experience. We bathed elsewhere or we didn't bathe at all.

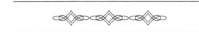

Meanwhile, we spent our nights doing one of two things — either partying or stealing. If we had drugs, booze, and money, we partied. If we didn't, we would go out and steal so we could party. Mostly we looked to steal cash, although we would take anything we could pawn off or trade for drugs.

With stealing being so easy in Japan, we had to be cautious about getting greedy. One time, before Tommy and I ran away, I learned my lesson the hard way when I got a little too overzealous at a chain department store in Yokohama. Big cities like Yokohama have stores built up instead of out, as is typical in the U.S. So a store the size of a Wal-Mart Supercenter would be tall and narrow — maybe eight stories high. If the merchandise you wanted wasn't on the first level, you took the stairs or elevator to the appropriate floor.

On this occasion, I was with two friends and looking to hit a musical instrument store on the fourth floor. We were all wearing black trench coats, which probably drew attention to us. Still, it was not as much as one would think. Trench coats were in vogue in Japan and guys with long hair, earrings, and trench coats didn't arouse much suspicion in the music section in the days when heavy metal was king and musicians looked pretty outrageous.

We took the elevator up to the fourth floor and then quickly went into action. Our modus operandi was simple: Two of us would stand watch, while the other stuffed merchandise under his trench coat. Then we would switch roles, and the next guy would load up.

Normally, when we hit a music store, we went for guitar pedals or miniature V-neck guitars (which happened to fit very nicely under an arm), but this time we were going for guitar tuners, guitar cables, and tablature books — those thick music books that show the reader, in meticulous detail, exactly how to play the music by a particular artist.

We all took a turn stuffing merchandise under our coats and then took the stairs down to the ground level, because we figured that taking the elevator down might look suspicious. When we got about 30 feet from the door out to the street, I thought we were home free. Then three Japanese men in suits started yelling and running after us.

My two friends were smart. Instead of running into the street they ran *back* — up the stairs and into the music store. I thought they were being stupid. "What are you doing? Don't run back inside, get out!"

I ran outside, and, of course, all three men followed me. With the security guards preoccupied with me, my two friends went back to the fourth floor, surreptitiously returning everything they had stolen. As a result, they didn't get caught. They walked out of the store scot-free.

Meanwhile, I labored under the weight of all the merchandise I had under my coat. I had a dozen or more tablature books, a half-dozen battery-operated guitar tuners, and a half-dozen 15-foot guitar cables. As a result, it didn't take the security guards long to catch me. I was only a block away from the store when one of the guards caught up to me and grabbed me by the back of my neck and hair. Then another one yanked me up by my pants and underwear, just like a wedgie. I was busted with close to $800 worth of merchandise on my person.

When the police arrived on the scene, they took me downtown and threw me in jail. Believe me, it's no fun to be in jail in a foreign country where you don't know the language and police protocol. I had heard stories about Asian countries where you would get caned or beaten for stealing, and I started imagining the worst.

As soon as the arresting officers put me in a cell — luckily an isolation cell without other prisoners — the jailers started yelling at me in Japanese. It can be intimidating when you don't know what they are saying. I had no idea what was coming next. I was thinking, "Help. ... Somebody. ..." I feared that they would just dispose of me somehow, and I would never be heard from again.

As it turned out, I was only locked up for about half a day. The police located a man who could communicate with me in broken English. Through him, I happily gave the police my parents' phone number at Atsugi. When my mom and dad heard what had happened, they immediately jumped on a train and came up to Yokohama to bail me out.

When my parents arrived at the police station, I was never so happy to see them in all my life. Not because I wanted to see them, but because they were my get-out-of-jail-free card. When they arrived, I knew that I was going to get out without getting beaten or killed.

Before I was released, the police told my parents that I could keep everything I stole, assuming they paid for it. From my cell, I overheard my mom cry, "But that's exactly what he wants. We're not going to pay for it and then let him keep it! Translate that!" she urged the interpreter. When he did, the police nodded emphatically as if they had suddenly come to the realization that she was right.

It was a long, awkward train ride back to the base. There wasn't a whole lot of conversation between us, but my parents gave me a lot of disappointed looks. My parents were probably thinking, "Donnie's behavior can't possibly get any worse than this." Well, it could, and it did.

It wasn't long afterwards that I ran away with Tommy. And my behavior in Japan, well, that was nothing compared to what I did after I got kicked out of Japan, went to my first rehab, and then moved back in with my Catholic parents.

7

ROAD TRIPS

AFTER HAVING BEEN KICKED OUT OF JAPAN and then after having completed my first stint in rehab in Pennsylvania, I moved back home with my parents who were guardedly optimistic that my most troubled days were behind me. They held out hope that I would mend my wicked ways, return to school, and perhaps even begin going to church with them. While churchgoing was certainly out of the question, I begrudgingly agreed to go back to school, if for no other reason than it was the best place to meet girls. I had little interest in continuing my formal education, but there was no way around it. If I wanted to meet girls my own age, I had to attend school.

During my sophomore year, I made a concerted effort to drag myself to class almost every day. Yet no matter what I did I never felt like I belonged. I certainly didn't fit in with my classmates, most of whom were focused on academic achievement, being part of a sports team, or participating in student government. My interests were pretty much limited to getting drunk or stoned and listening to music. I missed Japan so much, and living in Reading, Pennsylvania, was a totally different world.

Looking back, I realize I was like most alienated teenagers, except like everything else I took teen angst to the extreme. By the time I was 16, I was convinced that my parents and teachers would never understand me. I felt like I needed a new family.

Eventually, I became so disenchanted with school and so frustrated by living at home that even the lure of pretty girls couldn't keep me there. Although I didn't officially drop out of high school until the 11th grade, for all practical purposes, I had emotionally checked out long before then. My attendance record during my junior year was so abysmal that once, when I showed up for homeroom, the teacher gave me an astonished look and exclaimed, "Oh, you still go here? We assumed you had moved away."

I finally dropped out of school once and for all at the age of 17, not long after I found what I believed might be my new family — the so-called Deadheads who followed the Grateful Dead. In an unlikely musical turnabout, I switched my musical focus from heavy metal to hippie music virtually overnight.

Actually, like most overnight sensations, my infatuation

with the Grateful Dead's music was a couple of years in the making. I was first exposed to the Dead while I was in rehab. But at the time, their songs didn't resonate with me. It seemed like their music was geared toward peace-loving hippies who wanted to be one with nature. When I was 14 or 15 years old, I wanted fast, heavy music that mirrored my own anger and aggression.

But as soon as I started to do a lot of hallucinogenic drugs like mushrooms (psilocybin) and LSD, I started to get what the Dead was all about. While I never totally turned my back on heavy metal, I found it difficult to listen to metal while I was high on acid or taking mushrooms. The two just don't go together. When you're on a hallucinogenic, you want to hear music that's slow and soaring — a song like Pink Floyd's "Comfortably Numb," where you can hear guitarist David Gilmour squeezing the juice out of every note.

The other thing that appealed to me about the Grateful Dead was that their songs were pseudo-philosophical. Unlike many hard rock tunes, the lyrics weren't about being angry or being ticked off at your parents. They were about love and finding something. It seemed the Dead were always singing about a road or a path. At that time, feeling alienated and like I didn't fit in, I desperately needed someone to show me the way.

It also didn't hurt that I could identify with many of the protagonists in the Dead's songs, who always seemed to be gypsies or drifters. All the moves and all the changes in my life made me feel like I was a drifter, too. And in songs like "Tennessee Jed" and "Alabama Getaway," they would sing about the places I wanted to go. It was almost as if I had written the lyrics and Jerry Garcia and Bob Weir & company were singing them for me — or even to me. I wasn't alone anymore.

I had the same feelings about Bob Marley and reggae music. The lyrics seemed to be geared to me and my struggles and problems and my wanting to break free and be left alone. I wanted nothing more than to live outside any rules and regulations — to love who I wanted to love, to lust after who I wanted to lust, and to live a kind of cosmic togetherness with drugs, girls, and music.

My positive feelings about the Grateful Dead only intensified after the first time I went to a show. I vividly remember the experience. It was at the Spectrum, the old home of the Flyers and Sixers on Broad Street in downtown Philadelphia. I recall being incredibly high and never having experienced a show like that. All the concerts I had previously been to had a totally different feel.

At a typical rock concert, you would feel like one among many, and you left as one among many. The atmosphere didn't necessarily bring you closer to other people. Oftentimes, there'd be a mosh pit where the fans would get violent—kicking, punching, and thrashing around. Getting knocked down, losing an article of clothing, and getting a bloody nose or black eye, that was almost a badge of honor. But it didn't necessarily bring you closer to others.

A Dead concert was just the opposite. It was a great communal experience with Jerry Garcia leading the way. Instead of "we're here to rock you!" the band was there to take you places. Jerry seemed to have a natural gift for leading everyone in this transcendental experience. You felt like you were uniting with people you didn't even know. During the show, you would literally be hugging and embracing people you had never even met before.

Even the Dead's musical approach was unique. The band never played the same sequence of songs at a concert; the set list changed with every performance. And instead of short pre-rehearsed songs with prescribed guitar solos, the band would go off on 20-minute jam sessions, improvising as they went along. One never knew where the band was headed or where the music would take you. Everyone in the audience would be dancing around so free, so you'd walk away from the show thinking how close you felt to everyone around you. It just gave you this feeling of being welcomed and being loved. Let me tell you from personal experience — it was a lot different than being stomped on in a mosh pit.

After that show at the Spectrum, I started going to as many Dead shows as I could. And in doing so, I started making friends with other Deadheads — the kind of people whose entire existence revolved around following the Dead from show to show and city to city. These people would essentially live out of their car, often a Volkswagen bus — the vehicle that everyone still associates with Deadheads — selling food and homemade trinkets as a means of supporting themselves. That basically meant making enough money to buy a little food, a lot of drugs, and the requisite Dead tickets.

One of the new friends I met had one of these VW buses. That bus was a party on wheels — outfitted with a wine rack, beanbags, and thick shag carpeting, making it a very inviting place to lie around and get stoned. I did some serious partying on that bus.

In fact, I did so much LSD and so many mushrooms when I was a Deadhead that I have few memories of my travels. How we got to many of the cities — or even found our way to the arenas — I have no idea. How we got money for food and gas is an even greater mystery. I was so high all the time that I don't even remember very many of the concerts. It's still amazing to me that we didn't have a fatal accident in that bus or get busted for drug possession.

Of course, a lot of the time we didn't even get in to see the concert itself because we didn't have tickets. Even though the Dead usually performed for two or three nights in each city, there were never enough tickets available to meet demand. So like a lot of other Deadheads, we would have to content ourselves with tailgating before, during, and after the show. Beforehand, anyone without tickets would walk around the outside of the arena, saying, "I need a miracle!" Translation: "I need a ticket." That was the slogan for Deadheads. But if you weren't fortunate enough to experience a "miracle," then you'd spend the entire evening tailgating outside.

That meant that even after 20,000 fans staggered inside an arena to see the Dead play, there would still be thousands of people outside in the parking lot — cooking, smoking, drinking, doing drugs, having sex, or maybe all of the above. One could walk from bus to bus in the parking lot, and everyone you'd meet would be an instant friend. One minute you would approach someone you'd never met before. The next you would be sitting around a little fire, and they'd be telling you their life journey. Then they'd play you a song they wrote on their guitar or give you a bootleg of a past Dead show. You would walk away marveling at how friendly everyone was and how welcome you were, even among strangers.

During the entire period I was a traveling Deadhead — six months or so — I had no means of financial support. I bummed food and drugs from other Deadheads, taking advantage of whomever I could and then moving onto the next person. In essence, I was a 17-year-old homeless person, and I certainly looked the part. By this point in time, my hair — which hadn't been cut in a very long time — was down to my waist. As best I can remember, I lived on potato chips, Doritos, Mountain Dew, and marijuana brownies. I was skinny and out-of-shape and generally wasting away.

Still, in my mind, I was living exactly the life I wanted to lead. I believed that the hallucinogens were enriching my life, allowing me to experience a whole different dimension of thinking. I would get so stoned that I could *see* the music.

But in reality, who knows what I was thinking? There were times that I did so much LSD that everyone looked like and moved like a turtle. In those days, I was so stoned out of my mind that I don't even know how I sustained life.

One night in particular comes to mind: I was in rural Pennsylvania with two of my Deadhead friends, and I remember us starting the evening at his house, drinking beer and doing LSD together.

I don't recall exactly what happened after we went out, but at some point, we must have ventured to a local tattoo parlor. That became clear when I woke up the next morning and shuffled off to the bathroom only to discover that I had the Grateful Dead's "Steal Your Face" insignia — a skull with a lightning bolt going through it — on the back of my left shoulder. I had no idea it was there until I turned on the bathroom light and looked in the mirror. Whoa, that was a surprise!

Alarmed, not to mention hung over, I woke my two

friends to ask how I got the tattoo. Only then did I discover that we had *all* gotten tattooed. My friend John had a tattoo on his arm and his girlfriend had one on her ankle. Naturally, mine was the biggest and boldest of the three. But none of us could remember where we went or how we chose the designs. It remains a mystery to me.

To this day, I still have that tattoo. I've kept it because it's such a vivid reminder of my past — it makes it seem *real*. It's a daily reminder about where I've been and how far I have come.

I know that it's possible to get a tattoo removed, although it's a painful and expensive procedure that usually leaves a scar. But in all honesty, there's something about it that seems to make a difference when I'm evangelizing. Listeners often do a double take when they hear that I have a Grateful Dead tattoo. In some small way, I think it adds authenticity to my message — that I'm not exaggerating about my past and in particular about my time with the Dead.

During my Deadhead phase, I often found myself in the unfortunate position of having no money and no place to stay. Sometimes there was simply no one available that I could "use" for food and shelter. In that situation, I had no choice but to return home, just so I'd have something to eat and a place to sleep. Somehow, my parents always found it in themselves to take me back, although they were usually furious with me for running off, and rightly so. But I never could stand being home for long. The minute I lined up a new place to stay or a friend to bum around with, I would be back out on the road.

It was during one of those brief stays at home that my mother approached me and said, "Donnie, why don't you go to church with us?" I just looked at her with my usual blank stare and replied, "Are you nuts? Have you completely lost your mind? Me, go to church? No way. Church is for the weak. It's for the losers who are looking for some false hope when there is none. Church is a joke and a lie. I can't believe you and Dad have been suckered into believing this nonsense."

The truth is, I wasn't interested in any organized religion. The Grateful Dead was my religion. The Deadheads were my family, and Jerry Garcia was my leader. I didn't need anything else.

To this day, I'm amazed and humbled that even though I had for all practical purposes renounced my parents and wouldn't stay at home unless I absolutely had to, my mom and dad didn't stop providing for me. In the midst of my comings and goings, my parents were nice enough to buy me a used car — an Oldsmobile sedan. Most 17-year-olds have to beg their parents to buy them a car, usually as a reward for working hard or doing well in school. Here I was just about the worst son in the world, and my parents still gave me one. It was an old person's car — the kind you'd see Grandpa and Grandma puttering around in — but I didn't care. For the first time, I was self-sufficient in the sense that I could now get from place-to-place on my own.

As soon as I got the car, I drove down to my grandfather's house in West Virginia, hoping to live with him for a while. I knew I couldn't live with my parents, but I'd always liked the wilderness of West Virginia. I hoped living with Grandpa might provide some stability in my life. My grandfather agreed to take me in, but the local high school didn't. I made a half-baked effort to enroll, but the school administrators resisted. One look at me and my transcripts, and they knew I was going to be trouble.

Again, my grandfather's house was in a very rural area, and I simply didn't look like I belonged there. The guys who went to this school were all country boys. They wore overalls and flannel shirts and NASCAR T-shirts. They weren't used to seeing a guy with hair down to his waist, wearing tie-dyed pants and a Deadhead T-shirt. The school principal asked me, "Why do you want to come to school here? We're not sure this is such a good idea."

But when my grandpa got wind that the school didn't want to enroll me, he got mighty upset. And Grandpa was not the kind of man you wanted to tick off. I had seen him get upset before, and I thought he might get physical with the principal.

Luckily, the school relented and accepted me on a trial basis. As it turns out, they needn't have bothered making a fuss. I never went back to school, anyway. Instead, I preferred to wander the streets of small-town West Virginia, searching for a joint and a pretty girl.

Unfortunately, when I made the decision to move in with my grandfather, I had conveniently blocked out the memory of how dull life could be for a teenager in rural West Virginia. Within a month or two, I started to go out of my mind. Don't get me wrong, it was certainly better than living with my parents. But on some levels, it was even more frustrating.

One of my biggest complaints about living in rural West Virginia was that there were few girls around. In my boredom, it wasn't long before I went back to drinking and consumed all of my grandfather's alcohol. But I didn't really want Grandpa to know I was drinking his booze. One time, he had a six-pack of Pabst Blue Ribbon in the refrigerator. I craved a drink but was fearful about how he would react to me taking his beer. So I opened one of the cans, drank half of it, and then put it back in the fridge. When he discovered the open can, he said, "Who the hell drinks half a beer and then puts it back it the fridge?" I was busted.

The absolute worst thing about the three months I lived with Grandpa is that I rarely had any marijuana to smoke. At one point, I became so desperate to get high that I went out into a neighbor's corn field and shucked a few dozen ears of corn. No, I wasn't interested in eating fresh corn on the cob. I shucked only for the corn silk — the hairy-looking stuff at the top of each ear — because I heard that if you smoked enough of it, you could get high. The process turned out to be too labor-intensive for my taste. I had to shuck a lot of corn and smoke a lot of silk to get a good buzz.

One of the few positives that came from living with Grandpa is that I had the chance to meet my biological father. My grandfather and uncle thought it might be a good idea for us to get reacquainted, so one day my uncle arranged a meeting. In a certain sense, it was like meeting him for the first time. You see, the last time he had seen me, I was an infant.

The downside is we didn't hit it off too well. As soon as we saw each other, we both went into a state of shock. I thought to myself, "Good grief. This is my dad?" I got the same vibe from him, as if he was thinking, "Good grief. *This* is my son?" I saw him as a hillbilly, and he saw me as a long-haired hippie freak. And we were both right.

But we soon got over our initial discomfort. Since getting divorced from my mom, he had remarried and had both a son and a daughter. And he told me about my grandfather, grandmother, and other relatives I had never known. While not a warm and fuzzy reunion, it wasn't unbearable either.

After a few months living with my grandfather, I decided to take off. My natural restlessness kicked in, and I had to go somewhere else for a while. As it happened, during the time I was staying with Grandpa, I was picking up a lot of hitchhikers in my Oldsmobile. One of them I got to know quite well, an unemployed stoner who lived nearby with his wife and infant son. He had been prodding me to take him to Philadelphia to show him around the city. I was at my wits' end in West Virginia, so I agreed. He told his wife we were going to Pennsylvania to look for work, and we shuffled off to Philadelphia for four days.

We never looked for work, even for a minute. We went to Broad Street and South Street and partied and chased girls, my stoner friend being quite the accomplished womanizer. I was so drunk and so stoned for the entire trip that I hardly remember anything from those four days. But the ride back home to West Virginia was quite memorable, even though we were both drunk on a bottle of Red Grape Mad Dog — a cheap fortified American wine also known as Mad Dog 20/20.

When we got on the Pennsylvania Turnpike just outside Philly, we were issued the usual ticket from the toll booth operator, the kind that states the cost of the toll at each exit along the Turnpike. We didn't think to tuck the ticket in the sun visor or some other memorable place; we just threw it on the floor and went right on drinking our Mad Dog.

Of course, as we continued down the Turnpike, we eventually came to a sign that read: "Toll Booth: 2 Miles." But as we approached the toll, neither of us could find the ticket. We both started getting agitated, knowing that if we couldn't produce it, we'd have to pay the maximum toll, which amounted to close to 10 dollars.

About a half-mile from the toll booths, I pulled the Oldsmobile over to the side of the road to give us time to do a thorough search of the car. While we were stopped, we realized that we not only didn't have the ticket, we didn't even have the $1.75 we needed to pay what we actually owed.

So my friend — just as drunk as I was on the Mad Dog — ordered me to get out of the car. He wanted to drive. I let him get behind the wheel. As soon as he merged back onto the highway, he floored the accelerator. In seconds, I realized what he was going to do. At first, it seemed like a good idea, but as we got closer and closer to the toll booths, the space we had to squeeze through started to look smaller and smaller. We were moving so fast that the dashboard was rattling and shaking.

Then, all of a sudden — *vroom* — I heard a swooshing sound. We were through. We had just run through one of the toll booths at 95 miles per hour. Thank goodness the toll collector didn't jump out of the booth, and thank goodness no one crossed our path because, if they did, we would have killed them instantly.

We were laughing and whooping it up as my friend took the first exit after the toll. We figured if we took country roads the rest of the way home, the police wouldn't be able to catch us. Plus, we'd avoid having to pay any more tolls on the Turnpike. We defied the odds once. I wasn't sure we wanted to push our luck.

The irony is that about a mile from our destination, our luck finally ran out. My friend was so drunk that he lost control of the car and slammed it into the side of an overpass going about 30 miles per hour. We both started laughing after we crashed. We had sped through a toll booth at 95 miles per hour and come through unscathed, but out here on the open road, we had just crashed into a bridge abutment. When we staggered out of the car, we realized my Olds was messed up pretty bad. So we pushed it down a nearby embankment and into a field.

The next day, when I was sober, I called my biological father and told him what had happened. He came out to meet me and towed the car back to his house. Since he was an auto mechanic, I figured if anyone could fix the car, he would be the one.

But when he looked at it, he said, "What's the point?" Before the accident, the car was only worth $1,200 or so. Now one of the axles was bent, and we had damaged the flywheel. Plus, there was a lot of structural damage to the front end.

I offered the car to my dad. "Whatever you can salvage, go ahead and sell," I said.

With no home and now no car, I feared I might have to return to my parents again. If worse came to worst, I knew they would take me back — despite the fact that I had totaled and abandoned the car they bought me — but I hoped it wouldn't come to that.

I started looking for an apartment near where my biological father lived, figuring shelter was a higher priority than replacing the car. It didn't take me long to find a place, although it was nothing to write home about. It was so small and insignificant that it didn't even warrant a full address; the address was 17-and-a-half Main Street — the other "half" belonging to the apartment next door.

Needless to say, it was a dark and dirty place. The neighbors weren't exactly fine upstanding citizens either. The man who lived next door to me — in the other "half" — was a construction worker who smoked more marijuana than I did. Inside his apartment, big bags of marijuana were lying around everywhere, some of which he had grown in his closet. His girlfriend was equally memorable; she walked around topless all day. It was all so hillbilly.

For better or worse, my stay at 17-and-a-half Main was short. After I lived in the apartment for three weeks, I came to the realization that the first month's rent was about to come due, and I didn't have any money. Yes, I was so irresponsible that I wasn't even aware you had to have a job to pay your bills.

After pondering my next move for a few days, I decided that my best bet was to get out of there before the landlord came calling. I called up my friend Adam, one of my Deadhead pals who lived in Pennsylvania. He agreed to take me in for a little while.

At that point, I simply got up and abandoned the place. Not only did I never pay the rent, I left the place in shambles — food, pizza boxes, and garbage everywhere. I even stuck the landlord with a huge phone bill. I didn't give it a second thought.

In many ways, Adam and I were very similar to each other. We didn't share the same outlook on the world, but we had the same likes and interests and the same challenging home life. We also enjoyed the same music and shared a passion for fishing. But mostly we bonded over our shared interests — namely, girls and drugs. In many ways, Adam was very similar to my friend Tommy in Japan in that he was very impetuous and off-the-cuff. We would talk about doing something together. Then we'd do it that night or perhaps the next day. We'd just do it, whatever it was. And I thought that was so cool.

Another reason we bonded together is that we could also identify with each other's misery. Adam was also a high school dropout and had a horrific relationship with his parents. I remember going over to his parents' place one day, and a very intense shouting match started as soon as he opened the door. Like me, he, too, wanted to get as far away from home as possible.

So just like I had done with Tommy, whenever we got blitzed together, we would fantasize about moving somewhere where no one could hassle us. One day, we saw pictures of Oregon in a *National Geographic* magazine and impulsively decided that it was where we wanted to be. The magazine came with a map and had all these awesome pictures of the rugged Oregon coast. It looked like a hippie paradise, with surfing and everything. In our drug-addled minds, our dream started to take shape: We would move out West and live in Oregon.

Of course, we had no idea how we were going to get out there or where we would live. But we loved the idea of moving somewhere where no one could find us and no one could bother us. We dreamed that we could grow an endless supply of marijuana and live off the land. The idea was to find a few pretty, nature-loving hippie girls and live on the Oregon coast for the rest of our days.

The only hitch in our plan was that Oregon was more than 2,500 miles away, and I no longer had a car. That meant if we had any chance of getting from Reading, Pennsylvania, to the West Coast, we'd have to utilize Adam's — a car that was neither operational nor street legal. He had somehow acquired a long, low-riding Pontiac that seemed to be held together with duct tape. It also had a Confederate flag sticker on the roof — just like the General Lee in the *Dukes of Hazzard*. This meant that it would attract a lot of attention outside the Deep South, not a positive attribute, especially since we would frequently be drunk or stoned when driving around.

Our first challenge was to steal enough parts to get the engine running. Adam was an exceptional mechanic who was very creative when it came to improvising solutions to mechanical problems. Within days, he got the engine running. Next, we needed to have music for our trip, so I went out and stole a car stereo and a CB radio. Now we could listen to our music and communicate with truckers. Lastly, we needed the car to look street legal, so we went out and stole registration and inspection stickers.

We were good to go — sort of. The car still had its challenges. For one thing, Adam couldn't keep the car from overheating. So if we were driving for an extended period, we would have to drive around with the heat on, kind of a challenge in the summer, even if we had all the windows rolled down. You see, driving with the heat on was the only way to keep the car from overheating.

Of course, we regarded this as a minor inconvenience, not something that would wreck our plans. Adam threw a big roll of duct tape in the trunk, and we were off to Oregon. That is, as soon as we found a way to get gas and food for the trip.

I suggested we make the short drive to my biological father's house, thinking it would be a place to stay temporarily. We might even get the opportunity to do work projects for relatives to make a little bit of traveling money. But my idea was a total bust. We only ended up staying for a few days because work projects and drugs were in short supply, hardly a surprise considering that most of my family was on welfare.

Our next stop was Spencer, West Virginia — a very rural section of West Virginia. Adam knew a logger who had a cabin there, but when we arrived, this logger friend was nowhere to be found. There wasn't much in the cabin, just a stove and two beds. But that was good enough for us. We stayed for two weeks, listening to our music and smoking dope all day long.

When it became clear that Adam's logger friend wasn't going to show up anytime soon, we decided to head West and hope for the best. The trip went smoothly, for a few hours at least. But as we drove west through Kentucky on 1-64, the car broke down. What were we going to do? Adam pinpointed the problem, but we didn't have the money to buy the parts to repair it. We managed to push the car into the parking lot of an auto parts store. Then we begged customers for the money to buy parts. Eventually, we raised enough money to purchase what Adam needed for repairs.

But the breakdown led us to doubt the ability of our Cheech & Chong mobile to get us where we were going. We had plenty of marijuana and stolen cassettes to play on the car stereo but not much else. We had a car that was prone to mechanical problems and no money for fuel. Every time we needed gas, we had to pull into a gas station, fill up, and then peel away. It's a miracle we were able to do that without ever getting caught, because this car was by no means built for a quick getaway.

I suggested we take yet another detour, this time through Memphis, because I had a friend from Japan who was living in nearby Bartlett. When we got to western Tennessee, we looked up my friend in the phone book and showed up on his doorstep unannounced. My friend's mother answered the door. When she saw it was me, she turned white as a sheet. With her intimate knowledge of my past behavior in Japan, I was about the last person she wanted to see associating with her son. Since we weren't welcome in the house, we slept in the car for a few days while partying with my friend. But it quickly became obvious there was no future for us in Bartlett. Adam suggested we move on, this time to New Orleans, where Adam had a cousin.

Our revised plan was to get temporary jobs in New Orleans, save some money, and then continue on to Oregon. It's a seven-hour drive (400 miles) from Memphis to New Orleans, but it took us three days to get there. That's because Adam kept insisting that we stop at all the Harley bars we encountered along the way.

We were so out of place at these bars. Maybe it was our old, beat-up car parked next to all these big motorcycles. Or maybe it was because we weren't leather-wearing locals and didn't have the prerequisite beards or boots.

But the bikers never bothered us. They could see we weren't a threat to their good time. The best thing about those places is that we didn't have to buy our own drinks, a good thing since we were underage. In bikers bars, most everyone knows everyone else, and a biker will buy a round for the house. Then someone else will buy the next round. Most of the time, we didn't even know who was buying our drinks. We would get blasted while these bikers were out on the dance floor with their women — down south jukin' to Lynyrd Skynyrd or the Marshall Tucker Band. When we had our fill, we'd leave and go on to the next place.

We also picked up a lot of hitchhikers on the way down to New Orleans. There wasn't really any reason for us to do so, except for the adventure of the experience. Most of the guys

we picked up were homeless. By the time we got to wherever it was they wanted to go, we were happy to see them off.

When we got to New Orleans, we made a beeline for Adam's relatives' house. Once again, we showed up on a doorstep unannounced. In this case, his aunt answered the door. Once again, the reaction was a state of shock. Adam asked if it would be okay if we stayed while we looked for jobs, but his aunt and uncle were very reluctant, no doubt owing to our unkempt appearance and exceptionally bad manners. In the end, they broke down. We were told we could stay for one week, and that was all. Then we'd be back out on the street, whether we had found jobs or not.

During the day, we went out ostensibly to look for work. But instead we rode around, listening to Credence Clearwater Revival (CCR) and cruising for girls. It's silly, but the only reason we were listening to CCR is because we believed they were from Louisiana. Only later would I find out CCR actually hailed from northern California. Meanwhile, we managed to behave ourselves. But when the week was up and neither of us had found a job, we were back on the road.

As it turned out, Adam had another cousin who lived in New Orleans, and she was about our age. We went to her trailer home where she lived with her husband. And because they also enjoyed drinking and smoking marijuana, they agreed to let us stay there with them for a while.

Of course, both Adam and I desperately needed jobs if we were going to have any chance to raise enough money to make it out to Oregon. Adam's cousin worked as a cashier at a Piggly-Wiggly supermarket, while her husband was employed by a tugboat operator on the Mississippi River. Despite the fact that I didn't have any skills or work experience, they helped both of us get jobs with their respective employers. One of us could work on a tugboat and the other at the Piggly-Wiggly.

After a night of particularly heavy drinking, we decided to flip a coin, with the winner choosing whichever employer he preferred. Having won the toss, I opted for the tugboat, mostly because I didn't want to work anywhere called Piggly-Wiggly. I couldn't imagine myself walking around a supermarket wearing a name tag and providing all those people with customer service.

A few days later, I went on my job interview. I had to lie to get the job, claiming that I had past experience working on a tug. Adam went on his job interview the same day, and miraculously, the Piggly-Wiggly hired him as well.

As for myself, I couldn't believe that anyone would give me a regular job. Adam had had a few jobs before, so hiring him was plausible, even reasonable. But I had no skills and didn't even want to work. I just wanted to be a bum, but I wanted to get paid for doing it. Believe me, with all the pot and alcohol I was consuming, I had no business working anywhere, much less being responsible for securing barges up and down the Mississippi River.

To this day, it amazes me that our tugboat wasn't involved in a major disaster. The captain, who was responsible for steering and giving orders to the crew, did lines of cocaine while operating the boat. For the most part, I stayed below deck, smoking marijuana, cooking catfish, looking at pornographic magazines, and planning how I was going to spend my first paycheck. I was getting paid double the minimum wage, so it figured to be a decent amount of money. It wouldn't be the kind of money I became accustomed to in Japan, but it would be more cash than I'd seen in a while.

As for my responsibilities, every once in a while, the captain would blow the horn. It was my signal to come on deck to tie off a barge by wrapping enormous cables around some anvils. Of course, I had no idea how to tie off a barge, so I tied the knots as if they were shoelaces. Before long, the knots would come apart. Then the captain would come over and tear into me. He would yell insults like, "You stupid hippie!" Luckily, no barge ever came completely free of its moorings. Otherwise, it might have floated downriver and crashed into a bridge.

Adam's experience at the Piggly-Wiggly was less eventful. Mostly, he just had to stock shelves and help customers find what they were looking for. He wasn't getting paid nearly as much as I, but his work wasn't as stressful either.

Two weeks into our respective jobs, we celebrated my first paycheck by having a big party at the trailer home. We were having such a good time that we ran out of beer, so I volunteered to head down to the Piggly-Wiggly to replenish our supply. When I got there, I went inside, pulled two cases of cold brews from the beer case, and then boldly proceeded to run out the front door. I didn't even try to be discrete about stealing the beer.

Security immediately followed me out of the store, while the manager called the police. A police cruiser must have been in the area because, before I knew it, I was being chased by a police car, its lights flashing and siren wailing. When I heard the siren, I dropped both cases of beer and ran as fast as I could until settling into a dark corner near a bank. I sat in this corner for what seemed like an hour. Because I was so drunk, probably all of two minutes passed by before I decided to get up to try and find my way back to the trailer park.

That was my first mistake. As soon as I stood up, the bright beams of a police car shined in my eyes and an officer shouted, "Freeze!" When two officers came over to apprehend me, I gave them a hard time, screaming obscenities at them and trying to break free. That was my second mistake. They pushed me against the side of the squad car, and one officer frisked me while the other read me my rights.

During the search, they found my double-edged butterfly knife. I had had no occasion to use it since bringing it home from Japan. But after the officers uncovered the knife, they regarded me as even more of a threat. Still, I was lucky they didn't find everything I had on my person. A quarter-ounce bag of marijuana and a pipe saturated with resin occupied one of my front pockets. Those could have easily warranted additional charges.

The officers put me in their squad car and drove me to downtown La Place, a suburb of New Orleans adjacent to Metairie. After the police booked me, they took a mug shot and threw me in a cell with five other men. I'll never forget what the officer said when he locked the cell behind me: "Welcome to your new home." The scariest night of my life was about to begin.

8

THE HIPPIE DREAM

AS THE POLICE OFFICER ESCORTED ME to the holding cell, it suddenly hit home what a bad situation I had put myself in. Being in prison in Japan was frightening, but this was worse. Much worse. At least in Yokohama, my parents were only an hour or so away by train and could come to rescue me. This time, my parents were 1,500 miles away, and they weren't even aware I was in Louisiana, much less locked up in jail. No one was going to come rescue me from this mess.

Even if I could somehow swallow my pride and call for help, the best-case scenario would involve my dad flying to New Orleans in the morning to bail me out by the afternoon. I'd still have to spend at least 12 or 15 hours in the holding cell.

There wasn't much of a chance that Adam would bail me out either. Adam's association with me would most likely cost him his job. The Piggly-Wiggly manager was aware that Adam and I were friends. And even if the supermarket didn't let him go, he hadn't yet received his first paycheck. With only a few dollars to his name, how could he come up with enough money to secure my release?

My mind raced as I tried to think of anyone else who might be able to get me out of this jam. Adam's cousin and her husband came to mind, but I wasn't optimistic about that prospect. To begin with, they never seemed to have any extra money. Plus, the fact that I had stolen from Piggly-Wiggly, her employer, didn't work in my favor either.

I was face-to-face with the reality that I was a scrawny kid with hair down to my waist, about to face the night with five of the biggest, toughest-looking dudes I had ever seen. Three of the five were African-American; two were white. All of them were at least six feet tall and ripped. Either they were day laborers or they spent a lot of time lifting weights at the gym. They all wore jeans, T-shirts, and work boots, so I guessed they might be construction workers. It wasn't clear to me whether they knew each other or whether they were strangers.

When the cell door clanged behind me, I didn't bother to introduce myself or say hello. The first thing I said — to no one in particular — was, "I'm going to *kill* that cop." I figured if I effected a nasty disposition, no one would bother me. But my tough-guy act wasn't working, and I knew it. Worse, they all knew it, too. Straight away, one of the men looked at me and growled in a menacing voice, *"Tonight, you're mine."*

"Help," I thought. I didn't know exactly what my cellmate meant, but it sounded threatening and perverse. I made up my mind right then and there that if the men tried to assault me, I was going to fight back. I was going to do whatever I had to do to avoid being touched. If one or more of us didn't leave the cell alive, so be it.

My biggest fear was of all these guys getting together to gang up on me. If that were the case, I'd have virtually no chance of fending off an assault. Almost as disconcerting, I was still so drunk that I couldn't maintain my balance, which made me an even more inviting target.

Another thing I immediately started to worry about was going to the bathroom. I still had a lot of beer in my system and desperately needed to use the toilet. Much to my chagrin, the one and only toilet in the cell wasn't sectioned off or behind a partition. If I had to go, I would have to do it in plain view of these five men. I decided after the "you're mine" comment, there was no way that was happening. I would simply have to hold it in for as long as I could. I didn't care if my bladder burst or I got constipated. I wasn't going to open the door to any trouble.

I ended up staying awake for the entire night, doing my best to look both mean and intimidating all the while. But the combination of trying to stay awake and fight off the need to go to the bathroom was more than just uncomfortable; it was downright painful. Morning didn't bring any relief, only an additional inconvenience — a bad hangover.

I was never so happy when the sun rose and that night was over. I started to sober up and began thinking about what I would say to my parents when I called them. I wasn't sure about police procedure, but I assumed I would get to make one phone call. After all, that's the way it was on TV. I resigned myself to the fact that I would have to reach out to Mom and Dad.

Around 10 a.m., a police officer came down to the holding cell and called out my name. I wondered why he was calling on me. Was it time for me to make my phone call? Was he going to give me the chance to go to the bathroom in private?

"I guess you said your prayers last night because one of your friends has paid your bail," said the officer in a thick southern accent. I was shocked and relieved at the same time. I wouldn't have to worry about calling home, after all. And as unlikely as it seemed the night before, it looked like I was going to get out of this cell unscathed.

When I was safely on the other side of the bars, I considered taunting or insulting my cellmates. But on second thought, I decided I was better off playing it safe. After all, if they didn't release me and I had to return to that cell, I would have kicked myself for not keeping my mouth shut.

When the officer took me upstairs, he was all business. After I went to the bathroom, he advised me of the charges I faced — and informed me that I had to return in a few weeks for my court date. Otherwise, a warrant would go out for my arrest.

He then handed me my wallet and identification and advised me to be on my way. I quickly noticed that one of my possessions was missing. "Where's my double-edged butterfly knife? I want that back, too," I demanded. The officer sighed and told me I wouldn't be getting it back. He told me some nonsense about how it was illegal in Louisiana to carry a knife with a blade longer than six inches, and that if I was smart, I wouldn't press the issue. Otherwise, he would be more than happy to charge me with possession of a deadly weapon. In reality, the dude probably just wanted my knife for himself.

I cursed and muttered to myself as I walked away. The "law" seemed absurd. "What's the difference between a three- and six-inch blade?" I wondered aloud. I was bummed about losing the knife. Even though I didn't use it very often, it still had a lot of sentimental value.

My demeanor brightened a bit when I saw Adam, who was waiting for me in the station lobby. "Thanks for bailing me out, dude," I said, as soon as we made eye contact. But my attitude quickly soured when Adam recounted how he got the money to post my bail.

Earlier that morning, Adam had collected all of my music cassettes and hauled them down to a local pawn shop, one that was conveniently located just down the street from the police station. As soon as the shop opened its doors, he pawned off all my music. Then he hightailed it over to the station house to fill out the paperwork necessary to effect my release. My cassettes, as it turns out, were worth just enough to set me free.

Yet as soon as Adam told me what he'd done, I totally went off on him. "How could you sell all my music?" I cried. All I could think about was the loss of my precious tapes. In the span of about two minutes, I went from being eternally grateful to yelling at him for selling my personal belongings.

In hindsight, it seems the police took pity on me for being drunk and acting like an idiot. They certainly didn't cite me for every law I broke. Between the knife and the drugs they didn't find, the charges could have been quite a bit more substantial, because I took more than a few swings at the arresting officer.

Nevertheless, I now had a court date in Louisiana hanging over my head, and I wasn't especially keen about hanging around for my day in court. Suddenly, I had the need to get as far away from New Orleans as possible. So the next day, when I woke up, I said to Adam, "Let's just go to Oregon right now." I didn't really consider the consequences of skipping out on my court appearance. I figured by the time I was due in court, I'd already be in Oregon. The police would never find me if I was living all the way across the country in the back-woods somewhere.

At the same time, I realized if we were going to make a break for it, we would need supplies for the trip. And we would need them fast. The easiest thing was to take whatever we could from Adam's relatives, so that's what we did. The next day, while his cousin and husband were at work, we rummaged around their trailer home and packed up whatever we felt might be useful to us. We took food out of the refrigerator and cherry-picked from their music collection. Then while we were packing up the Cheech & Chong mobile, we peeled the registration sticker off a nearby car and lifted the car stereo. Basically, instead of saying goodbye to the people who were kind enough to put us up and get us jobs, we robbed them blind.

We didn't get far before I began to have second thoughts about our plan. Looking at the distance on the map, I started to get the feeling we weren't ever going to make it all the way to Oregon. It dawned on me just how far it was to the West Coast and just how difficult it was going to be to cross the Rockies in a car held together with duct tape. As soon as we crossed the border into Texas, I proposed heading back to Pennsylvania. Adam admitted he was kind of thinking the same thing.

The hippie dream was dead. Or so it appeared.

As we set a new course — now heading east on I-20 — I advocated returning to West Virginia as quickly as possible. Part of my rationale was self-preservation, because I was paranoid about the possibility of getting picked up by the police. We were driving a beat- up, old car with bald tires and a broken tail light—both obvious safety hazards. Plus, we were sleeping in the car at night, either at truck stops or at visitor's centers on the highway. The police had plenty of excuses to stop us, either for safety violations or for parking illegally.

Adam, however, was unconcerned about the possibility of getting pulled over. At one point, we were driving down the highway while drinking a 12-pack of beer and Adam insisted on stashing the empties in the rear window. "Dude, that just doesn't look good. Are you asking for trouble?" I cried. Adam was calm as could be, but every time I saw a police car, my heart would jump because I assumed they were looking for me.

The other part of my rationale was that I wasn't ready yet to give up on our hippie dream. Maybe we couldn't get to Oregon, but we could live a similar lifestyle in West Virginia. All we had to do was to go someplace where no one would bother us. Adam and I settled on driving to my biological father's place, if only because he had a spread of land big enough where no one would find us.

As soon as we got there, we drove deep into the woods, where we parked the car in a field and set up camp in a hollow. The only supplies we had on hand were a tent, tarp, shotgun, ax, and a fishing pole — all borrowed from my father — as well as a car battery and a huge supply of marijuana and Kraft macaroni and cheese.

We hooked up the car battery to our tape deck. Then, for two months, our lives revolved around listening to music, getting stoned, and cooking a box of Mac & Cheese when we got hungry. In order to pass the time and get some exercise, we cut down trees with the ax, an acre-and-a-half worth of trees in two months. It's not like there was anything else to do. After cutting down a tree, we would chop it up and start a fire. The next day, we would repeat exactly the same routine. It was an earthy, hardcore existence, but it made us happy. There was no one to bother us, and I didn't have to worry about getting busted by the cops.

I'm not sure how long we would have continued living this extreme lifestyle if we didn't run out of marijuana and macaroni and cheese. But a shortage of food and drugs finally motivated us to leave, in search of more food and drugs, of course. We finally drove back to Pennsylvania, the place where we had started many months earlier, no better off than when we had left.

Not long after we returned to Pennsylvania, Adam's blatant disregard for caution finally caught up to him. On the way to obtain weed from one of his dealers, the cops pulled him over and arrested him for possession of narcotics. I wasn't with him that particular evening, thank goodness, because the police would likely have discovered my outstanding arrest warrant. After the police busted Adam for the drugs, they realized his car had stolen plates and registration, not to mention an expired inspection sticker. They immediately impounded his car and threw him in jail.

I was bummed out about this unfortunate turn of events, but it never dawned on me to try to help him. I was so selfish that I didn't even consider trying to bail him out, as he had done for me just a few months earlier. When I heard that he'd been arrested, I said, "Wow, that's a tough break." Then I went right back to drinking my beer, without giving him a second thought. I haven't seen Adam since and have no idea what became of him. He was just another disposable friend in a long line of disposable friends.

Adam's arrest did have one immediate impact on my life. It forced me to move back in with my parents. I hated living with them, but with no job and no source of income, I had little choice. Despite the fact that I was going nowhere and nothing was working in my life, I just couldn't seem to change my ways. In fact, the worse things got the more drugs I did. I was caught in a vicious cycle with no end in sight.

My quality of life deteriorated even further when I started doing crack. Like just about every other drug I tried, I didn't like crack the first time I used it. But after I learned how to properly use a crack pipe, I found that I loved it. Even before I started coming down from the high, I would be thirsting for more.

Before long, I found myself willing to go anywhere and do anything to get crack. On one occasion, I even found myself in a crack house, crawling around on the rug on my hands and knees looking for any cocaine that might have fallen on the floor. There were cockroaches running around and maggots in the sink from all the unwashed dishes. A crying baby could be heard, unattended in a back room. Yet there I was on the floor, right along with the baby's mother, searching frantically for white specs on the floor. If we found anything white, we'd put it in the bowl and smoke it, even if we didn't know what it was.

We did this for hours until I became so paranoid and so distraught over the baby's crying that I literally ran out of the house and into the night. I spent the rest of that evening hiding under a thorn bush, where I thought no one could hurt me.

One day, not long after my crack house visit, I remember coming down off a high and hearing voices. The voices were asking me, "Are you okay? Can you hear me, son?"

As soon as I heard the voices, I started thinking, "Where the heck am I? What's going on?"

When I opened my eyes, I found myself lying in a bed surrounded by men and women in white coats, all looking at me intently with concerned looks on their faces. When I tried to move, I realized I was strapped down and wearing a hospital gown. I had the taste of vomit in my mouth and felt absolutely wretched.

"Where am I?" I whispered.

"You're in a hospital," a male voice replied. "You'll soon be on your way to a drug rehabilitation facility where they will take good care of you."

"Whatever," was all I had the strength to mutter back.

A few hours later, I was indeed committed to an institution. Being in rehab once before, I understood what was happening to me. But I could tell right away that this rehab was going to be an entirely different experience than the first time around. I felt as if I had suddenly been dropped onto the set of *One Flew Over the Cuckoo's Nest*.

A quick tour through the facility would reveal patients padding around in silence, their eyes glazed over, as if they were in a trance. Others had anxiety disorders and screamed or squealed *constantly*. And I mean constantly. Some of the patients were such drug addicts that they had literally fried their brains. Their incoherent ramblings would periodically be punctuated by shouts of "Yeah, man! I hear you!"

Being committed to a bona fide nuthouse certainly got my attention, at least for a fleeting moment. I remember thinking, "I do not want to end up like these people, so I better get my act together. Fast."

But the shock value of these psychotic nuts diminished quickly, and my concerns dissipated within a day or so. As soon as I met some of the other teenagers who were in with me — particularly the girls — I went right back to my old way of thinking. I bonded with my fellow druggies by telling war stories about all the drugs I did. Together, we fantasized about the kind of parties we would have when we were discharged.

In the meantime, I had no choice but to go along with the program. For the most part, I followed the guards' orders, obeyed curfew, and dutifully attended both group and individual counseling sessions.

Every so often, though, the regimentation became too much for me to take. On one occasion, my parents came in for a four-way counseling session, including myself and a counselor. I got so upset during the session that I tried to storm out of the room. "You're all out to get me!" I screamed, as I started throwing my fists at security. The guards tackled me and carted me off to a padded room, where they let me vent, pounding on and kicking the walls — for 45 minutes. When I finally exhausted myself, they took me out, and I resumed my daily routine.

In some sense, this second rehab was much more effective than my first experience, if only because I stayed clean for the entire duration of my stay. Owing to the high security, it was impossible for any patient to smuggle drugs into the facility. But ironically, it only made me want to make up for lost time. Almost from the day I arrived, I imagined the drugs I was going to do when I finally got out.

Perhaps then it should be no surprise that even after a full summer in rehab, my drug use picked up right where it had left off. The day I was discharged I told my parents that I was going to spend that first weekend with a friend from the institution — that we needed each other's support and that we were going to attend Alcoholics Anonymous (AA) and Narcotics Anonymous (NA) meetings.

Instead, we drove around in my friend's Camaro, blasting Eric Clapton's "Cocaine" while smoking a joint sprinkled with coke. We poked fun at NA and joked that we would be better off going to a Sexaholics Anonymous meeting where we could meet girls. Naturally, I came home completely blitzed, hours after our meeting was scheduled to be over. In one night, my parents' hope that I would stay sober was completely shot.

Nevertheless, my parents still refused to give up on me. A short time later, they advised me they were planning to move back to Norfolk, Virginia. They asked if I wanted to move with them. "Yeah, I do," I said. I was looking for a change, but I simply didn't know how. Somehow my habits always led me back into trouble. Norfolk was where my whole ordeal had started 10 years earlier, and I thought the change of scenery might help — that it might help me break out of the rut I was in. I was wrong. Again.

9

BURNING DOWN
THE HOUSE

S HORTLY BEFORE MOVING BACK to Norfolk in 1991, my parents made the decision to buy a second home in West Virginia, where they planned to live after my dad's eventual retirement. My parents would spend an occasional weekend there, fixing up the house in preparation for its eventual use as their permanent home.

Although my mom and dad enjoyed the process of remodeling this second home, having a weekend getaway also had a secondary advantage — namely, it allowed them to get away from me, their unemployed, drug abusing, slacker son. For a few days, every six weeks or so, my parents and my brother Matthew would escape all the pain and aggravation I caused them. It was a chance for them to recharge their batteries, so they'd have the energy to deal with me when they returned.

One ordinary Friday afternoon, as my parents were packing for one of these weekends, I got the brilliant idea to host a party. Normally, I didn't like having friends over at my parents' house — I preferred to go out rather than stay in. But for some unexplainable reason, on this particular day, I felt the urge to be the center of attention. I wanted to be known as the guy who had hosted the mother of all parties — a guy who really knew how to show everybody a good time.

As soon as my parents pulled out of the driveway that Friday evening, I got on the phone and started calling all my friends. "Dude, I'm having a big party tomorrow night," I said. "Why don't you come over?"

My friends sounded enthused about the idea and that got me even more pumped. After I spoke with all my friends, I started calling casual acquaintances — people I only knew through AA or NA meetings. If I was going to have a bash, I wanted to have more booze and drugs than anyone ever thought possible.

But when Saturday afternoon rolled around, I started feeling insecure about the prospects for a large turnout. Doubts started to creep into my mind. "What if nobody shows up? What if people don't have a good time?" I got so stressed that I decided to try soliciting additional guests and drove around the neighborhood, periodically sticking my head out of the window and yelling, "There's a party at my house tonight! Bring all your friends!" That was my message for anyone and everyone whom I encountered on the street.

Much to my surprise, when I pulled back into the driveway early that evening, there was already a big crowd of people loitering outside the house — all waiting to get in and have a good time. I had never seen most of them before, but they were kind enough to bring kegs of beer and claimed to have lots of drugs. So I let them inside, and we started partying.

Right away, someone went over to the stereo and started cranking CDs from my mom's collection — including songs like "Superfreak" by Rick James and "Celebration" by Kool & the Gang. The music got everyone pumped up. Before I knew it, my houseguests were dancing around, ordering pizzas, and doing lines of cocaine on the coffee table. I thought it was so cool. "This is going even better than I expected," I beamed to one of my friends.

The first indication that I had pushed things too far came when one of my parents' neighbors — a devout Christian — showed up on the doorstep all red-faced and looking like he was going to pop a vein. When I came to the front door, he immediately began questioning me: "What on earth is going on here? Are your parents home, young man?"

Before I could answer, someone came up behind me and started telling this poor man off, cursing and screaming at him to leave us alone. The confrontation drew the attention of others. Before I knew it, a whole group of us were berating my neighbor, telling him he was a loser and that he should shut up and go home and pray. He threatened to tell my parents if we didn't turn the music down, but that didn't discourage my visitors. A threat like that only made them want to turn it up louder.

The discussion ended when someone walked over and threw a cup of beer near the neighbor, and he walked off in disgust. Obviously, we weren't going to let anyone get in the way of our good time, much less a cantankerous, religious neighbor.

A few minutes later, the party was cranked up a notch when one of the partygoers who had been doing lines of coke in the living room suddenly went into convulsions. One second, he was high as a kite and having a good time; the next, he was face down on the floor convulsing. No one knew what to do. And no one cared. We all stood there thinking he was dying, but no one offered any assistance. Thank God, he didn't die.

Yet, somehow, even the sight of watching a guy O.D. didn't dissuade me from doing more drugs. When one of my friends pulled out a couple sheets — double dip — I did LSD with him. But by the time I began tripping, I started to feel uncomfortable.

The entire house was now filled with inebriated partygoers. There were people doing immoral things everywhere. Guys were raiding the refrigerator for food; a girl started banging out a tune on the piano; I saw guys pouring unfinished drinks on my mom's houseplants. Things were getting out of control, and I started feeling powerless to put a stop to it.

The breaking point occurred when one of my friends came in from outside and told me that a guy was pouring gasoline all over the floor of the carport. I immediately ran downstairs and into the garage, only to find that someone had indeed emptied the contents of my dad's five-gallon gas can.

In fact, the puddle completely encircled my dad's car. Worse, the garage door was open and there were guys smoking cigarettes in the driveway, casually flipping their ashes right next to this highly flammable pool of gasoline. I immediately started screaming, "What are you guys doing? Are you crazy? Don't flick your ashes *here!*" Even in my drug-induced haze, I knew if I didn't act immediately, there would soon be a ring of fire burning around my dad's car.

The guys in the driveway stared back, looking incredulous. They were like, "Dude, what's wrong with you? Calm down."

But I was long past the point of being able to calm down. Watching strangers trash my parents' home while I was tripping on LSD became too much too take. I started to freak out.

I slammed the garage door closed, then ran back upstairs, and started screaming, "Everybody get out! Just get out!" Naturally, everyone turned to me to see what all the fuss was about. Knowing that I was on LSD, people just attributed my tantrum to the drug and ignored me.

"Dude, *he's having a bad one,*" I heard someone say, indicating that he thought I was having a bad trip.

But the fact is that I had lost control of the party, and despite being high, I still had sense enough to know that it wouldn't be a good thing if my parents' house burned to the ground.

Most of my guests regarded my tirade as a buzz kill. Within a few minutes, I had driven all but a few visitors out of the house. The only people who stayed were a couple of acquaintances and a girl I was interested in. After spending some time with the girl, I went downstairs to watch TV.

I got a blanket, curled up on the couch, and started flipping through the channels, looking for nothing in particular. When I saw Jack Nicholson and Shelley Duvall on the screen, I put the remote down and sat straight up. I didn't really want to watch *The Shining*, but I couldn't stop myself. I was riveted.

Yet the longer I watched the more I started having a bad trip. Now *I really was having* a bad one. I became so tense that my muscles tightened and my jaw locked up. I felt the walls of the house closing in on me. I was bugged out.

At some point, one of the guys who remained in the house came downstairs and stood watching me with a drink in his hand. I didn't recognize him, but he was like, "*Dude? Dude?* Are you alright?" I was paralyzed with fear and could barely move.

But by around eight or nine in the morning, I started to come down from my trip and managed to trudge down the hall and into the bathroom. On the way there, I got my first inkling of how much damage the house had sustained. In the hallway, I found vomit on the walls and on the carpet. I wondered what kind of shape the rest of the house was in. When I went upstairs, I found the girl. She was still passed out. Otherwise, no one else seemed to be around.

Panic began to set in as I stumbled back downstairs to check on the rest of the house. The damage to the common areas was even worse than upstairs. Much of the living room furniture my parents had brought back from Japan and the Philippines was damaged — the bamboo shredded and broken. There were cigarette burns and red wine stains on the rug and couch.

Even worse, the very expensive Yamaha piano my parents bought in Japan was seriously damaged. There were big dents in the wood, one of the legs of the piano bench was broken off, the seat was cracked, and smokers had used the interior as an ashtray.

As for the entertainment center, the TV was still intact, but the VCR, stereo, and my mom's CD collection had all disappeared. Even our family dog, Max, a Siberian husky with one blue eye, was nowhere to be found.

My last stop on this mini-tour of destruction was the garage, which was largely intact —except for the big puddle of gasoline, of course. My parents were supposed to be home in six or eight hours. How on earth was I ever going to clean all this up?

I decided I would tackle one or two rooms at a time, so the job wouldn't seem quite so overwhelming. First, I ran to the supermarket, where I bought a big bag of kitty litter, which I put down to absorb all the gasoline in the garage. The kitty litter was an ingenious solution, and before long the garage was back to normal, except for the fact that it reeked of gasoline.

Next, I went upstairs to tackle the bedrooms. I stripped the beds and stuffed all the sheets and pillowcases in the washing machine. I started filling garbage bags with the cups, empty bottles, and cigarette butts that were lying around. I started to think I was doing a good job of cleaning and that maybe the house wasn't such a disaster area, after all. Of course, I was fooling myself. My judgment was still clouded from the aftereffects of the booze and LSD, and my efforts weren't as productive as I imagined them to be.

However, while cleaning the hallway and the bathroom, I began to realize how bad it was. The vomit just wouldn't come off the walls and out of the carpet. In fact, scrubbing just made things worse. I ended up leaving streaks of puke all over the white walls. Eventually, I resigned myself to the fact that there was only so much cleaning I could do.

Early that Sunday evening, my parents returned, looking relaxed after their weekend away. But as soon as they saw the living room, reality set in and their calm was replaced by disbelief. They got more upset than I had ever seen them in my entire life. "I can't believe this!" was all I heard over and over again as they took stock of the damage. Making matters worse, I hadn't cleaned up quite as effectively as I thought.

Of course, while my parents were still reeling from the shock, our Christian neighbor came over. He was only too happy to fill them in about everything that had happened the night before, including how rudely he had been treated. Needless to say, my parents would never leave me home alone for a weekend again. And can you believe that even after that, my parents still offered to take me to Virginia with them!

After the move to Norfolk, Virginia, my father was assigned to an aircraft carrier, one making nine-month long voyages to the Mediterranean. I considered his assignment to be a good break for me, because it meant I'd only have one parent to contend with for a while. After the house-trashing incident in Pennsylvania, my relationship with my parents was more strained than ever.

After my dad went out to sea, I told myself I was finally going to change, that I was going to be a different person by the time he got back. But the change I was looking for didn't exactly materialize. One of my main goals was to hold down a job, which I thought might provide some stability in my life. I managed to get hired at a nearby restaurant, but the gig lasted less than a week. Every day, when the lunch crowd came in, I would get really irritated. The customers would have very specific needs, such as, "I'd like two squirts of ketchup, three of mustard, and two pickles, please."

My attitude was, "Whatever. I'll give you whatever I feel like." When I screwed up an order — which was all the time — the customers would yell at me or complain to the manager. After a few days of this, I said to the manager, "Take your stinking job. I don't want it."

Shortly after that, I took another job, this time selling cleaning products door-to-door. I tied my waist-length hair in a ponytail, put on a collared shirt, and away I went. Except as one might expect, I wasn't a natural born salesman. I would ring someone's doorbell, while hoping to sell a $100 bottle of cleaning solution, and my opening line would be something like, "I was just wondering if maybe you'd like to try this product I've got here?" My approach was all wrong from the get-go. In order to sell this stuff, you had to have the demeanor of a used-car salesman. The guy who trained me always came at the customer strong: "You haven't lived until you have tried this," he would say. I stuck with that job for a week, but I didn't sell a single bottle of cleaner. My mom was so disappointed when she found out I had quit. I had failed her and myself yet again.

Finally, hoping the third time would be the charm, I applied for a position at a movie theater — a brand-new 10-plex located just down the road from our house. For the first time, I found myself able to hold down a job. Mostly, it's because I got along famously with my colleagues. My boss was a 55-year-old Don Knotts-type character who partied like an animal and one of my co-workers was a crack user. I could relate to them.

While the movie theater gig was a small step in the right direction, I still felt like I was regressing. Most notably, as a result of my crack use, I ended up in a relationship with a girl who gave me a venereal disease. I was embarrassed because I had to have my mother take me to the hospital for treatment. I begged the doctor not to tell my mother what I had contracted. Luckily, because the prescribed medication was a lotion, I was able to keep my mom from finding out the exact nature of my ailment.

Between the house-trashing, venereal disease, and my drug use, I was experiencing so many terrible things that my life was becoming all-out darkness. I was nearly 20 years old but didn't feel like I wanted to live anymore. I wasn't exactly suicidal, but at the same time, I wanted to press the delete key on my life.

I had experienced every sensual satisfaction one could possibly have with women, I'd heard every kind of music, done every kind of drug, and at times I'd even had money. But in the end, it all seemed worthless. I always seemed to be back at nothing. Life sucked for me, and I didn't want to go on with the charade any longer.

10

THE DIVINE
2 x 4

ONE NIGHT, IN MARCH 1992, everything came to a head. I was at home, and as usual, my friends were calling and asking me out for the night. Typically, my friends didn't even have to call. I was already good to go. But on this evening, I refused all my friends' overtures. I didn't even offer them an explanation. I just wasn't into it.

My friends badgered me for a while, but eventually they got the message so the phone stopped ringing. I found myself sitting there alone in my room with nothing to do and no one to turn to. My existence was laughable. My life was a waste, and I was hoping it would somehow come to an end.

I didn't want to live, but I didn't know what to do about it either. I hated my life. I was restless and anxious about everything. I was so not at peace and thought that my life would soon be coming to an end, maybe even that night. I was scared. Terrified actually. I feared both life and death. Both sucked.

Yet I didn't want to be alone that night either because being alone by myself was torture. Plus, I got bored just twiddling my thumbs. One thing was for sure. If I wasn't going to go out, I needed to find some way to occupy my mind. Since I didn't feel like reading anything heavy, I thought I would try to find a magazine in the house, preferably one with a lot of pictures.

I went out into the hallway and scoped out my parents' bookshelf, hoping to find a *National Geographic*. There were all kinds of things on the bookshelf that I had no interest in, including encyclopedias and books on Japanese stuff. I looked for the classic *National Geographic* yellow binding, but I couldn't find it.

Then when I was about to give up, I noticed a book with a similar yellow spine. For an instant, I thought it might be a special edition of *National Geographic*. But when I pulled out the book and looked at the title, it read, *The Queen of Peace Visits Medjugorje*. I had no idea what this meant.

(Years later, I would find out that the alleged apparitions of the Blessed Virgin Mary in Medjugorje have not been approved by the Church and that Medjugorje remains a controversial topic. However, what is recounted in the following pages are the historical aspects of how that book helped change my life. The reader should know that it is not within my domain to determine the authenticity of Medjugorje, as that decision is left for the hierarchy of the Church alone.)

Now back to the story. …

Since there was a cross on the cover, I immediately associated the book with Christianity. As a result, I was immediately turned off by the prospect of looking at it, especially in light of an experience I had at a party about a year earlier. The party itself was typical of the house parties I attended at the time — lots of girls and drugs, accompanied by loud music. In the midst of this sensory overload, I found myself sitting on a couch in a dark room — tripping on LSD, of course — when I glanced over at the adjacent coffee table and saw *The Gospel of John*.

My first reaction was: "What is that doing here!" Then I started to freak out when the small book began to glow and radiate a very white light. Suddenly, I felt the need to escape. So I rushed outside into the yard — where I stayed for a long time, just looking up at the stars while trying to comprehend what I had just experienced.

Now, once again, I had a religious book in my hands, a book that I imagined to be the cult manual for my parents' religion. On the cover, there was a picture of a very strange looking woman. I thought to myself. "My parents read this, and they accuse me of being weird? This book is just stupid."

But since my evening was already shot, I decided to take the book back to my room to give it a closer look. I didn't actually want to read it. I only wanted to look at the pictures. I crept back to my room — making sure my mother didn't see me reading a religious book. Then I shut the door, sat down on the couch, and went straight to the pictures.

At first, none of the pictures made any sense to me. In one, there was a sad-looking, barefoot lady wearing all black, as well as a cross and an extremely rocky mountain. I couldn't understand why she didn't have shoes on, especially considering the mountainous terrain. There was a picture of six little kids on their knees, looking up into the air at nothing. Were they waiting for a spaceship to come and take them away or something? Was this some sort of religious *Close Encounters of the Third Kind*? I had to start reading the captions to the pictures to get a sense of what was going on. Apparently, the six children were having apparitions of something, someone, called the Blessed Virgin Mary.

"What's a Blessed? Who is Mary? And who is a virgin?" I wondered. None of it made any sense to me, and I began to question what my parents had gotten themselves into. This book was the most bizarre thing I had ever heard of, beyond the story of Bigfoot or anything one might see on TV. I was so curious I decided to start reading the book from the very beginning, compelled to find out exactly what kind of weirdness my parents were now involved in.

Of course, I was so ignorant that I couldn't even get past the cover jacket without getting confused. The author of the book had "Fr." in front of his name. Was that a typographical error? Did they mean "Dr." for doctor? I had no idea what the initials "Fr." meant. Even more strange was that the author had the initials "AA" after his name. I assumed he was a member of Alcoholics Anonymous. I thought perhaps that this author was actually trying to debunk religious theory.

Anyway, I began reading the book from the beginning and immediately didn't get it. There were saints, a guy named John the Baptist, and something called the Eucharist. My problem was that I knew virtually nothing about religion, let alone Catholicism. And, of course, this book was saturated with Catholic lingo.

I kept reading and kept coming across Catholic words, which I would try to pronounce aloud. Words like Blessed Sacrament, Eucharist, Holy Communion, Rosary, and scapular. All of these were foreign to my vocabulary, and I inevitably mangled the pronunciation as I attempted to verbalize them. There were so many words and phrases that I just didn't understand.

But as I continued reading, I became extremely fascinated with it. These six kids, who I didn't know, said they were seeing somebody from a place called heaven? What was heaven? For me, heaven was in the music I heard, as in Led Zeppelin's "Stairway to Heaven." Heaven was being next to a beautiful girl and smoking a joint. To me, heaven was a place that people sang about, but no one really believed it existed. The odd thing about this book is that heaven wasn't described as a mythical place. It was real.

It never crossed my mind that hell might actually exist either. To me, hell was a myth, too, a concept designed to scare people away from having fun — to make them act like dorks and nerds. In my mind, hell was a happening place, where all the girls were pretty and wanted to have fun, a place where everyone was high and stoned. AC/DC referred to it all the time in songs like "Highway to Hell" and "Hell Ain't a Bad Place to Be." Even the Grateful Dead referenced it in "Hell in a Bucket," singing, "I may be going to hell in a bucket, but at least I'm enjoying the ride."

In short, the message in this book was a real revelation to me, in clear categories of black and white. There's heaven and hell and right and wrong? There's truth and falseness, as well as light and darkness? Although it took me a few hours to comprehend it, I had never heard a message so clear as the one I was reading.

In a certain sense, I had always felt there was a certain yes or no to one's existence. After all, I always believed that my extreme behavior made me authentic in the sense that I was uncompromising when it came to authority. You were either authentic or not. There was no middle ground.

This book showed me a side of things I had never really heard of or experienced before, but I certainly could relate to the radical nature of the message. As I read more and more, I was attracted and repulsed by the message at the same time. It wasn't long before I realized this book was presenting me an offer to change my life and surrender to something greater than myself — to believe in God and be different. It was a revelation that required a revolution in my thinking. Could this be the way out I was looking for?

"No," I thought. It's just not possible that I could be forgiven or change. How could someone so perverse, wicked, and lustful change? At the age of nearly 20, I was convinced that it was already too late for someone like me. And this thought scared me. I didn't know how to live or how to carry myself.

Again, I heard myself wondering, "How would it be possible for me to change or be forgiven?" As I continued to read, the answer became clear. The Virgin Mary was saying that people have to believe in God and have faith. They have to surrender and give their lives to her also, so she can present them to her divine Son.

When the story began referring to Jesus, I felt those old feelings of dread creeping in. "Oh, no. Here we go. Here's the part where I have to give my life to Jesus and give up everything and forget about having fun." I was feeling good about the story until Jesus came up.

Yet I found myself very attracted and captivated by this someone who I couldn't see —this Virgin Mary. There was no picture of her. There was a beautiful statue, but even I knew she wasn't a statue — that she was alive. The book said she was living in heaven, sent by God for sinners, for people like me who had gone off and were living sinful lives. Yet how was I going to give my life to Jesus? I hated Jesus!

The Virgin Mary was saying things that were so clear and captivating that I found myself moved and literally experiencing emotion in a deep way. This was a kind of emotion I hadn't experienced since I was a little boy who really loved his mother and wanted to make her happy. And yet the Virgin Mary was saying that she was my mother, that she was the mother of those who had gone astray and was calling us back to God, to Jesus. She made it clear that she was not God, but she was pointing to her Son and saying He is the Messiah, the Savior of the world. I found myself totally falling in love with this mother, this woman.

As I continued to read, I said to her in my heart, "I want to believe. I really do. You are piercing the little bubble of my world and offering me something more than I have ever heard. I need this." All I had ever been taught in school was that I was nothing more than an evolved monkey. In a strange way, I knew that I had always wanted to hear something different like this. That's why I always sought satisfaction in women and music and drugs. To me, there had to be something outside of time. Was it really possible that I was more than just a glob of cosmic goo? Now the eternal was penetrating into my little world and saying, "There is more. I'm calling you to it and revealing it to you."

What the Virgin Mary was asking for was this thing called conversion. And she talked about foreign things to me like prayer and fasting. I might not have known exactly what she was talking about, but I knew it meant a total giving of oneself to her, so she could bring me to Jesus.

Up until that moment, I found it impossible to open up to Jesus because I had the wrong impression of Him. I believed He was the divine crusher of life — that He knows how wicked I am, how we all are, and He was ready to snap us out of existence at a moment's notice. As bad a person as I was, how was I going to ever look at Jesus eye-to-eye? After all, all the preachers on TV said people like me were going to eternally roast in a lake of fire!

Society and television had so brainwashed me — communicating a message that God was not merciful — that I felt there was no way I could do this. But I was comforted by the thought of Mary. It would be through the call of a mother, His mother saying, "I know. It's okay. That is why I have come — because He sent me. You need me, and like a good mother, I will fix and clean you up and everything will be okay. God is calling you to Himself, but He knows you are very wounded and have a completely wrong understanding of Him. Thus, He has sent me to you to prepare you."

I realized this is exactly how it had to happen for me. It made so much sense. I kept reading and reading. Then I found a card in the book that said: "If you knew how much I loved, you would cry with joy." And there was another card inside the book that had Mary saying: "You don't have to change to love me; loving me will change you."

Although I was in serious despair about my life, as I read the book, I felt as if my heart was being melted. I hung on to each word like it was transmitting life straight to me.

All through the night, I read page after page. When I finally closed the book, it was early morning. I read and then re-read parts in an effort to "get it," to understand this incredible message.

Though I didn't really understand, I even tried to meditate on the messages I was reading. Every word seemed to be meant for me. Mary would say, "Thank you for having responded to my call." And "Peace ... pray, pray, pray. I love you. I am asking you to do this. I need this from you. Convert."

As I read, I knew I had to give myself to this thing Mary called "church." She always seemed to be leading or pointing towards it. I always imagined church as being oppressive, something that dominated your life and sucked all the fun out of life. I believed that was the role of the Church, so naturally I hated church, just like I hated Jesus. But if I was going to surrender to Mary, I had to believe her and give myself to Jesus and the Church. And even though I didn't verbalize it or speak it internally, somehow I knew I had to surrender to this Blessed Virgin Mary. She would help me to understand the real Jesus, the Jesus whom I never knew.

Early in the morning, when I closed the book, I said, "The message in this book is life-changing. I have never ever heard anything so amazing and convincing and so needed in my life." One might say that this was my first prayer. Whoever this Virgin Mary was, I believed what she was saying — that she was my mother and came from heaven for me.

11

OUR LADY OF VICTORY

IT WAS AROUND 5:30 IN THE MORNING when I finally closed *The Queen of Peace Visits Medjugorje*. Knowing that my mother would soon be coming downstairs for her morning coffee, I made the decision to stay awake until I could talk to her. Not that there was a chance I could go to sleep. My mind was racing with all that I had read and felt. When I heard her rustling around upstairs, I went to the bottom of the stairwell to meet her.

As soon as she came down the stairs, I said, "Mom, I've got to talk to a ... ." My voice trailed off. I couldn't say it. I was like pride incarnate. I simply could not make myself say the words.

Again, I said, "Mom, I've got to talk to a Cath ... ." I just could not say it. I could not get the words out. It was like the ultimate humiliation, a sign of need, and a religious one at that.

My mom looked at me quizzically and said, "Donnie, what are you trying to tell me?"

Finally, I blurted out, "Look, Mom, I have to talk to a Catholic *priest*, okay?" I remember feeling so humiliated. I couldn't believe I just said those words. I felt like the Wicked Witch of the West from *The Wizard of Oz* after Dorothy splashed water on her. In my mind, I started shrinking. I suddenly felt very small.

My mom's response? "Yeah, right," she said, as she brushed by me on the way to the kitchen. God bless her. She probably assumed I was trying to manipulate her. It was certainly a reasonable response, considering my long history of lies and deceit.

But this time I was serious. I said, "No, Mom. You don't understand. I read a book last night. That book is tripping me out!"

"Which book?" she said, raising an eyebrow at me.

I quickly retrieved *The Queen of Peace* from my room and asked her point blank: "Who is this Blessed Virgin Mary? What is this all about?"

At that point, my mom's jaw just about hit the floor. She didn't say another word. She ran to the phone in the living room and began dialing. I overheard snippets of a conversation between her and a priest, one who she had apparently awakened.

She said, "Yes, Father … . I know … . I apologize. I didn't mean to wake you. But you have to talk to my son. Can I bring my son over in a half an hour? She must have met resistance because she continued pleading, "Father, you don't know my son. *You don't know my son.* You have to talk to him right away." But the priest did not comprehend the urgency of the situation — the need for a meeting at 6:30 a.m., with no prior notice. In his mind, what could be so important that it couldn't wait a couple of hours? Unwilling to give up so easily, my mother called a second priest but got much the same response. "Can we put off the meeting until 8:30 or 9:00 a.m.?" he asked.

As she was dialing a third priest, I interrupted and said, "Mom, isn't there one of those … ." My voice trailing off much as it did before. I didn't even know what to call it. We were living at Norfolk Naval Air Station, and I didn't know if the place I was thinking of was called a church or a chapel. I said, "Isn't there one of those *things* just inside the main gate?"

Understanding what I was referring to, she looked me right in the eye and said, "Yes, Donnie. Run!"

I threw *The Queen of Peace* down on the couch and out the door I went. I ran all the way to the main gate, still wearing the same clothes I had worn the previous day. I ran past the barracks and past several groups of Marines, who were already engaged in their morning exercises.

When I finally got to the chapel, I was out of breath, hardly a surprise considering that I had a two-pack-a-day cigarette habit. I was stooped over, huffing and puffing, when I looked up and saw the sign over the door of the chapel, which read, "Our Lady of Victory." Yet I couldn't work up the nerve to go inside. I silently said to myself, "This is good enough for now. I'm not going into a church."

And at the same time, I was thinking, "I don't want any pretty girls seeing me go in a church." I glanced over to my left and noticed another sign that said, "Chaplain's office." I decided to go try that door. It was certainly less intimidating than entering a church.

As soon as I opened the office door — before I even knew who or what was inside — I screamed out, "Catholic priest!" drawing out the words for emphasis. My cry sounded awkward. I simply had no social skills and no idea how to present myself or ask for help. As a result, I was about as subtle as a sledgehammer.

All the people inside — most of them dressed in newly pressed, bright-white Navy uniforms — turned to stare. I even saw a few individuals poke their heads out of doorways to see what the commotion was all about. Many of them gave me a look I was all too familiar with: It said, "What are you doing here? Please don't steal anything from us."

I can't blame these folks for being suspicious. Considering my funky clothes and long, unkempt hair, I looked like I had just jumped the fence and was going to hold them up. They all looked at each other like, "Do you want to be the one that talks with this kid?"

I said, "Look, I'm serious. I need to see a Catholic priest."

One of the men cautiously approached me and said, "Who are you?"

I said, "My father is a naval officer out at sea right now, but I live here on the base. I need to talk to a Catholic priest right away."

I was escorted down a hallway where another man in a crisp, white military uniform introduced himself to me. He said, "May I help you?"

I said, "I just want to see a Catholic priest, man."

"I'm Father Callahan," he replied.

I said, "Father? What's that? Are you a preacher?"

"Well, yes," he replied, shrugging his shoulders.

I said, "Are you Catholic?"

He said, "Yes, I'm a Catholic priest. What can I do for you?"

Though I was disappointed that he did not look like Moses — I guess I thought a Catholic priest would have a long beard and a staff — I did expect he was going to act like one of those TV evangelists I had seen on television. He would put his hand on my head, knock me out, and then I'd be free. As if to tell him what I needed, I said, "I'll fall down and do whatever. Just work it!"

Out of embarrassment, he stepped back a few paces. I was talking very loud and people in the vicinity were staring at us. He said, "Please don't make a scene. Let's go back to my office."

When we reached his office down the hall, I took note of the fact that he left his door open, a prudent move considering my behavior. He asked me a couple of questions before I started dumping my life story into his lap. I poured out everything like a confession. I told him all my sins, problems, and difficulties, and all the horrible things I had done.

This poor priest was sitting there with his jaw hanging down to the ground. He had been listening to sailors' confessions for years, but he hadn't heard anything like the sorts of things this nearly 20-year-old was sharing. Here I was telling him all my sins and how shamed I was and how I wanted the Virgin Mary and her Jesus in my life. He was positively blown away. He could hardly speak. I think I totally freaked him out.

Unable to wait for a response, I started pestering him, saying, "What do I do? What do I do? I want to believe this."

He finally said, "Look, I've got some business that I need to attend to. I need to go celebrate Mass."

"Mass? What's that?" I asked, not knowing what he was talking about. To my non–Catholic ears, I thought he was going to go dance around in the air or something. That's what "celebrate Mass" meant to me.

He said, "Did you see the chapel, Our Lady of Victory? I'm going over there shortly and celebrate Mass. Are you willing to go over there and wait for me. Afterwards, we'll talk."

"Sure," I said.

"Please sit in the back," he pleaded before departing.

I left and made my way over to the chapel, excited about the fact that this priest was willing to continue our conversation later. At the same time, part of me was a little suspicious that he might call the police. After all, I just confessed some pretty horrible things to him.

When I approached the door of the chapel, I got that same queasy feeling I had earlier. There was just no way I could go into a church. I looked at the doorknob and was afraid to touch it. I felt like if I went through the door, the divine guillotine was going to come down and my life would be over.

At the time, I still had what I call hillbilly theology. God was the divine marksman, and He had a 30-ought-six and was just waiting to get a shot at me. As soon as I got in the crosshairs, He'd pull the trigger, I'd hear a blast, and it would all be over.

I knew I was a wicked man and did not belong in a church. Trying to go through the door was like stepping into scalding hot bathwater. I did it slowly and cautiously. Eventually, I stepped through the door and found myself safely inside.

And wouldn't you know it, as soon as I got inside, the door slammed behind me. It was shotgun-blast loud.

I turned around, and there were five Filipino ladies in the front row. When the door slammed shut, they all looked at me as one. I felt like crawling to the back of the chapel because I was a long-haired freaky thing and didn't want to scare anyone. These ladies were probably expecting me to come over and steal their purses. I thought they were all going to jump up and start screaming: "Evil is among us! Evil! Evil!" Needless to say, I went to the back of the church.

It was really dark inside the church — the only light coming from a handful of lit candles that were placed strategically in the front of the chapel on some table.

All of a sudden, one of the Filipino ladies started talking. She was saying words really fast and with a very strong accent. Whatever she was saying, she was leading the five other Filipino ladies. All I heard was a stream of unintelligible words, "Hail something. … Holy something. … Amen."

My first instinct told me to go get the priest and tell him the Filipino ladies were up to something. The lady who was leading would say something and then the others would respond — call and response. Further, the leader seemed to offer her response to their thoughts. It all seemed very strange to me.

Then, all of a sudden, the leader turned and addressed me. She was holding what appeared to be a shiny necklace in her hand. She said, "Young man, do you want to pray the next decade?"

I looked at her like a deer in headlights. "What?" To me, the word decade meant only one thing — 10 years. I gave her a look that said, "Lady, what on earth are you talking about?"

She thought she could make me understand by clarifying things for me. She held her necklace up higher, shaking it, and said, "But it's the second sorrowful mystery." Whatever. Since she didn't get anything out of me, she turned around and the group went back to what they were doing. Obviously, I now know they were praying the Rosary, but then I didn't have a clue. These ladies seemed to go on forever. After a while, I started wondering if the priest was ever going to show up. Maybe he had lied about celebrating Mass. Maybe he was with the police right now, giving them the low down on what I had told him.

Just then the lights in the church suddenly came on. The priest came in, dressed differently than he was when I had seen him just minutes earlier. It was almost as if he was dressed like some sort of hippie. He came in wearing a long, multicolored robe, making all kinds of gestures, which the Filipino ladies seemed to be mimicking. They would stand up, sit down, stand up, sit down. They would stick out their hands in response to his gestures. The ladies seemed able to tune into each other, so they did the exact same thing at the exact same time. It was almost choreographed. How did they know to stand at the same time and give the same response, I wondered? I had never experienced anything like this. In my mind, there had to be puppet strings. It was like mental telepathy.

As I watched, the ladies all knelt down, their hands folded just like the children I saw in *The Queen of Peace* book. They all focused their attention on the priest, so I did, too. Up to this point, I could not hear him clearly due to the feedback, but when he went to the table in the middle, there was a microphone that helped me hear him.

At one point, it became very quiet. He bent over what I thought was just a table, and he had this little white circle in his fingers. In a clear voice, he said, "Take this, all of you, and eat it. This is My body."

Then he lifted this little white circle up into the air. I

glanced at the Filipino ladies, and they looked like they were in another world.

The priest held the little white circle up for what seemed like forever. All of a sudden —this is very difficult to explain — it was pure power. This voice said to me — it was all I could hear — it said, "Worship!" I freaked because I didn't know where that voice came from, and it surely wasn't me. In an instant, some knowledge came over me that the priest was holding Jesus Christ, the Savior of the world. It seemed to me like time had stopped. Every fiber of my being was in total fixation on what I was seeing.

I knew immediately that this was Holy Communion — that this was the Blessed Sacrament, and I was in the presence of God. I understood God is so in love with mankind that He comes and makes Himself present in extreme humility — in what looks to be a little piece of bread. Except it's not bread anymore. It's a miracle. It's Jesus!

Oh, I didn't know the theology of it yet, but I knew it was true.

Afterwards, the priest repeated the same process with the chalice. He bent over the altar and said, "Take this all of you and drink from it. This is the cup of My blood, the blood of the new and everlasting covenant. It will be shed for you and for all so that sins may be forgiven. Do this in memory of Me."

Then he elevated the chalice. Once again, this power came upon me and all around and within me and said, "Worship!" And I did. I don't know how, but I just knew that what I was beholding was wine changed into the Blood of Jesus Christ, who is God. It was as though Catholicism 101 had been injected into me. I realized at that moment that I had to become Catholic no matter what.

Everything within me was so focused. This was the answer. This was truth. Something, some knowledge, had been given to me, and it had moved me into affirming it with all my will. And I now believed it.

Next, the priest left the altar, while the Filipino ladies got up and met him halfway. He held out Jesus to them. And he said, "The Body of Christ." And they said, "Amen." Each lady did that, and each went back to her seat, looking so in love. They all had their hands folded, so focused, so aware that they had just received the living God.

I was thinking, "You have got to be kidding me. You mean to tell me that this miracle happens where God comes and transforms a piece of bread to be His Body and wine to be His Blood, so we can eat Him?"

It dawned on me that since I was nine or 10 years old, I had put a lot of different things on my tongue looking for happiness. I had drunk a lot of different liquids looking for that eternal high, something that was *more,* something that would satisfy me forever. Here was the answer. God! And He had penetrated my world through the Virgin Mary and had drawn me to Himself and invited me to partake of His very self, the food that brings eternal life. And the drink that sustains. I was totally blown away.

After Mass was over, I went back to see the priest. Suddenly, I had knowledge not only of the Eucharist and the Mass but of so many other things in Catholicism that I just couldn't explain. God gave me this gift. I started to tell this priest all that I had experienced, and again he looked at me like he was in shock.

I questioned him: "Because you're a priest, has God given you the power to be able to say this Mass thing and make Jesus present? By God's love, are you able to make this little piece of bread to be the Body of Christ and this wine to be the Blood of Christ?"

He said, "Yes."

I shared with him how at this Mass, it was revealed to me what was going on. This was the answer, the meaning of everything. This was the meaning of time and of everything that exists. I was drawing analogies to the sun and how the sun gives life to everything we know. And yet on one level, it is really Jesus in the Eucharist who gives life to everything. And only the Eucharist sustains us; it's the bread of the holy. My emotions and affections were so in love with Jesus and Mary that I was flying high. I knew the Church was like a hospital for ill people like me. Jesus was the doctor and the medication. And it is all free!

Father was flabbergasted. He said, "How in the world have you come to understand all this in just 45 minutes, from when I talked to you before Mass and now?"

I said, "Father, that's not all. When I went into the church and found the Filipino ladies praying, I thought it was weird. But do you know what they were doing?" He nodded, "Yes, they were praying the Rosary." Thus, I wanted to learn the Rosary as soon as possible.

I also asked him about the individuals portrayed in the stained-glass windows. "Are those people that have totally surrendered their lives to God and are totally caught up in God and the Church?"

He said, "Yes, those are saints. We can talk to them and pray to them, and they will help us."

"So in a certain sense, they are my older brothers and sisters?" I responded.

"Exactly," he said.

"And those statues in the front of the church. Is one of those the Blessed Virgin Mary?"

He said it was.

I said, "That's a beautiful statue. How about the man on the other side?"

"That's the husband of Mary, but he's not the biological father of Jesus because Jesus' Father is God," he explained.

"And the worshippers were kneeling at Mass because that's God? That would make total sense because if you are in the presence of God, you should kneel."

The priest said, "Kid, you are blowing me away."

I said, "Father, I don't know how to explain this, but I just got Truth 101 injected into me. I suddenly understand all this and it makes so much sense."

He said, "I've been trying to convey this to sailors for years, and you get it in 45 minutes?"

"Father, I don't know what to tell you," I replied.

The priest advised me his schedule was already booked for the rest of the day, but he was very interested in continuing our dialogue. He asked if I could come back the next day. Of course, I agreed.

Then he said, "Before you go, I want to give you a few things."

He went over to the wall and took down a big crucifix. He told me to take it home and hang it in my bedroom.

Then he went over to another wall and took down a painting of Jesus. It was Jesus with a heart. The heart had a flame above it and a cross and Jesus was pointing to His heart and it was pierced. There was an open hole or wound. He was pointing to His heart and, at the same time, giving a blessing. The other hand was raised towards me.

Finally, he took a third illustration off the wall. I had no idea who it was. It was a picture of an old man dressed in white. I was so naive that I assumed it was a picture of the priest's grandfather. Of course, I would find out later that it was Pope John Paul II, a man I would come to dearly love.

I took these three items in my arms, thanked the priest, and then went back to the church. When I went into the church, there was nobody there. But in some very strange sense, I felt there was somebody there. As I looked around, I walked to the front and saw a big, gold box with a candle lit next to it. Then it dawned on me: "Oh, my gosh! I think Jesus is in there!"

I could just feel a presence there, and I felt so ugly that I just backed away, knowing this was holy.

When I went to the back of the church, I saw a small room that had a sign above it that said "Confession." I peered into the room and almost began to cry. I knew exactly what this was. The mercy room.

Yet it was all happening so fast. So I headed for the door and gave a last glance at the gold box before promising myself that I would be back.

12

DIVINE DETOX

WHEN I BUSTED THROUGH THE DOOR of my parents' house, my mom was still there, nursing a cup of coffee. She didn't ask how things went with the priest, although she did take note of the crucifix and pictures. It must have been surreal for her to see me with illustrations of Jesus and the Pope, considering that she was used to me coming through the door with drugs, alcohol, or stolen property.

I went straight to my bedroom and immediately proceeded to rip everything down off the walls — everything from my Grateful Dead poster to my Miss December centerfold. Then I got the impulse to take things a step further. I went back out into the kitchen and retrieved a half-dozen big, black garbage bags from under the sink. I hustled back to my room and began filling the bags with virtually all my possessions.

I began by throwing out all my music, pornographic magazines, and drug paraphernalia — everything from my heavy metal records to my collection of *Playboy* and *Penthouse* magazines to all my water bongs and pipes. I stuffed my blanket and almost all of my clothes into the bags. Even things that weren't inherently bad went in the trash.

In the end, I filled up six 30-gallon bags, dragged them to the front door, tied them off, and then heaved each one of them into the front yard. My attitude was, "World, if you want any of this, feel free to take it."

On the way back to my room, I spied my mother observing me. She didn't say a word, but she definitely had a look of wonder on her face.

I didn't know what to do next, so I quietly shut my door and then proceeded to hang the crucifix, the Sacred Heart of Jesus, and the picture of the Pope. Hanging the pictures took all of about 10 minutes. Now what?

I suddenly realized that I wouldn't get a chance to go back to speak to the priest for almost 24 hours. I started to panic because I couldn't conceive of being alone for an entire day. My life was usually characterized by distractions. Now I was alone with my thoughts, a prospect that made me very uncomfortable.

Then it dawned on me that I should pray — to talk to God and the Virgin Mary. But guess what? I still didn't know how to pray. Until earlier that day, I had never said a prayer in my entire life. I don't even remember saying a prayer when I was baptized.

I went back to *The Queen of Peace* to see if it contained any instructions. Unfortunately, there wasn't anything along the lines of *How to Pray for Dummies,* so I started by mimicking the kids in the book. When I opened to the pictures, I saw the children had something in front of them — a table with rosaries and pictures — so I pulled out my dresser drawer. Then I got down on my knees, rested my arms on the dresser, and folded my hands just like the children did.

"What now? Do I say, *Schazzam?* How does this work?" I wondered.

As I was kneeling, what I didn't realize was that in my desire to pray — and I was trying really hard, grunting and concentrating — my eyes had fixed on this picture of the Sacred Heart, which I had placed right over the dresser. I focused on Jesus' eyes, gesture, and Heart. I began to feel such emotion and love that I broke — literally starting to cry and cry and cry. Until that morning, I wasn't even aware that it was possible for a person to cry like that.

In fact, I started crying so hard that I could hardly breathe. I had to literally gasp for air because I was crying so uncontrollably. There were torrents of liquid coming out of my eyes. Before long, the clothes I was wearing were soaking wet.

I continued kneeling in that position for the better part of the day. In fact, I never stopped crying the whole time that I knelt there. I just kept looking at this gesture of love and forgiveness, knowing that it was His desire to enter my life, to love me, and bring me peace. It made me want Him so much.

Hours passed. I was oblivious to the fact that I was kneeling, that I should have been in pain from being on my knees for hours on end. But I just poured out my life to Jesus, telling Him I wanted to love Him, that I wanted to be forgiven, that I wanted a new life and was willing to do anything to have it. I told Him how much I had fallen in love with His mother and was grateful that He would give her to me to be my mother. And I was thankful that He would send her from heaven, so that I could hear this message of forgiveness — so that she could bring me to Him.

At one point, I even admitted that I had never really understood Him and was convinced that He hated me. I admitted that I used to believe He didn't exist. I poured out my life to Him.

After crying for many hours, I realized that I began to cry in a different way. It was what I call divine detox. God wasn't taking a band-aid approach with me. He was acting as the divine physician and operating on my soul. It was painful at first. But once the spiritual operation was in progress, I realized He was healing me and that He loved me and was restoring me. I felt an enormous sense of relief.

After that, I began crying tears of joy. I started to feel almost bubbly and giddy, almost like a child being tickled by his father. Suddenly, I was animated. I had life again and felt so much different. My body tingled all over. I was so wrapped up in Jesus that I became aware of how much I was loved.

Finally, sometime during that afternoon, I got up from kneeling. Then, at a loss for what to do next, I made the decision to go to bed. What had happened to me was so unbelievable that I just wanted to sleep. Then I would get up the next day and tell Fr. Callahan what I had experienced.

When I curled up on my couch — I didn't even have a bed in my room, only a couch — I was so at peace. But all of a sudden something below me and within me — this is very difficult to explain — knocked me out of my body. I literally felt as if I had left my body. My physical form remained on the couch, but my soul or spirit had left.

I was paralyzed and in a state of shock. I couldn't move my hands or any part of my body. I tried to scream for my mother, but I couldn't make a sound.

For a moment, I thought I might be going to hell — as if everything I had just come to know was suddenly being taken away from me; I had been such a bad person that I wasn't worthy of God's mercy. I was going to go to this place of eternal separation from everything I had just come to know as being true and beautiful and good. I had no idea what to do.

Then, with every part of my being, I managed to interiorly scream. I spiritually cried out, "Mary!" It was so strong and penetrating a cry, it seemed to echo throughout the cosmos. It was like a little boy screaming for his mother after he's fallen and been seriously injured.

All of a sudden, I was violently slammed back into my body with what seemed like the force of the entire universe. It was so violent a thrust that I expected my mom to come running into my room to check on me. Yet nobody came because no one heard a sound.

After I got over the shock of the impact, a feeling of peace overwhelmed me, a peace that was tangible. Then I heard a voice, the most pure feminine voice I have ever heard and ever will hear. It was within me, it was outside of me, it was like liquid love being poured over me. It was pure maternal love. It said, "*Donnie, I'm so happy.*" That's all I heard, but I knew who it was. Nobody called me Donnie but my mother. Nobody. I knew this was the voice of Mary, the Blessed Virgin Mary. I was so at peace that I felt like a little boy snuggled close to his mother's breast. I was so at peace, so loved, and so at rest that I went into a deep sleep. I hadn't slept like that since I was a young boy.

When I got up the next morning, I felt brand new. I truly believed that Jesus had heard my cry to Him through Mary and had bathed me in mercy. A transformation had taken place the day before. I was clearly — albeit, indescribably — different. My honeymoon with God had begun.

As my mom and I had breakfast together, I told her I planned to visit Fr. Callahan again that morning. Even though I still had my funky clothes, she couldn't believe the change in me.

After I left the house, I went straight to the chaplain's office. "I have to tell you what happened to me when I left here yesterday," I said, as soon as I saw Fr. Callahan. I told him how I knelt and cried all day and how I totally gave my life to Jesus — how I was willing to do anything for Him. I recounted my experience of being temporarily paralyzed by fear and how I had been overcome with peace. Then I shared how I had heard Mary's voice telling me, "Donnie, I'm so happy," and that I believed there was mercy for me.

Father Callahan was dumbfounded.

I said, "Father, I know this sounds very bizarre, but I can't deny it happened. Just look at me. I'm *different* now. I know my life is going to radically change. I'm standing up straight, and I don't crave the things I craved before." He couldn't deny the external changes; they were self-evident.

So right then and there, I began my conversion to Catholicism. I said, "Father, I have to become Catholic today. I cannot live for anything else because this is true. I really believe the Catholic Church has the truth. I want to be totally taken up with Jesus and with what He's all about."

Father Callahan tried to temper my enthusiasm, saying, "Okay, this is great, but converting to Catholicism is a process."

I didn't know that. I expected to able to kneel down and that a priest would lean over me and say, "Bang, you're Catholic." Kind of like a knight being knighted in the Middle Ages. I didn't realize it would be a long process.

But despite my long history of impatience, I wasn't in any way deterred. "Let's do it," I said. "I'm open to it. Whatever it takes."

From that day forward, I almost literally began living in church. Virtually overnight, I went from being afraid to set foot in church to feeling like it was where I was meant to be and nowhere else.

I wasn't employed at the time. So as soon as I got up in the morning, I would walk over to Our Lady of Victory on the base. From the moment they opened the doors, I would be there to go, sit, and watch Mass — still totally in awe of what I was seeing. I would watch people go up to receive Jesus and thought it was amazing. "I can't wait to do it myself," I thought.

And the Sacrament of Confession? I would sit and look at the door of the confessional, thinking, "If the world only knew." So many people in the world are broke and wounded, and they choose to deal with their problems through psychotherapy. They pay psychiatrists their hard-earned money, and they don't even get forgiven. I saw confession as being just as therapeutic but better. After all, it was free and offered God's forgiveness. "This is a deal-and-a-half," I thought.

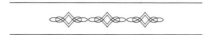

Going to church each day wasn't the only change I was going to make. Within days, I decided to cut my hair, and the decision was actually quite traumatic. I hadn't had a haircut in years. So, for me, losing my mop was a little like Sampson losing his strength. The hairdresser who I went to initially refused to cut it. When I sat down in her chair, she said, "No, no. I can't do it." I may have had a lot of split ends, but it still looked cool. Ultimately, I convinced her to go ahead — to make it quick, like she was ripping off a bandage.

When she finally cut it all off, I made a conscious decision not to keep the hair that had fallen to the floor. It was a symbolic gesture on my part; I felt like I had to let go of everything associated with the old me.

What's funny is that afterwards I experienced something similar to phantom limb syndrome, where someone who has lost a limb still feels sensations where the limb used to be. For months, I retained the habit of flipping my head back, as if I were trying to get my hair out of my eyes. Even though all my hair was gone, it still felt like it was there.

A few weeks after I got my hair cut, I was offered a job on the base working in the recreation department. I began spending my days cutting grass and maintaining the ball fields on the base, a mostly solitary job that allowed me to meditate and pray the Rosary even while I worked. I felt as if God was so providing for me.

The only downside was that because of my job responsibilities, I could no longer spend hours and hours a day in church. However, I was periodically able to attend Mass at the Immaculate Conception Chapel (the second of the two chapels on the base), which happened to be located across the street from the recreation center. On my lunch break, I would forgo eating, preferring to spend the time attending Mass. I would do the Stations of the Cross, pray devotional prayers, and kneel in front of the statue of Our Lady. And I loved every minute of it.

Meanwhile, Fr. Callahan, was reassigned to another facility, so I had to continue my conversion process at the Immaculate Conception Chapel. The priest there suggested that I familiarize myself with the process for becoming a Roman Catholic known as RCIA — the Rite of Christian Initiation of Adults. I started reviewing the materials he provided me, but I felt what I was reading was flowery. "This stuff is blah, man!" I complained to him. "Where's the hard-core stuff? There's no substance here." The materials didn't seem to address what Catholicism was all about. That particular RCIA didn't seem to get to the core of it all.

At the same time, I started doing my own research. What I discovered was somewhat discouraging. I understood that I was being called to be Catholic, but that I was being called during an extremely difficult time for the Church. It seemed a lot of people had their own ideas about what Catholicism should be or where it should be going or what it should and shouldn't be teaching. I learned of these alternate views from books and conversations with other churchgoers, many of whom seriously disappointed me with their lack of zeal for the faith. The things I heard people say made me wonder, "Are they really Catholic? I can't believe they are saying these things."

Despite my recent indoctrination, I already understood that the teachings of the Church are eternal truths and that they are never going to change. I knew nothing was going to change the Church's stance on abortion, contraception, or homosexuality. But when I discussed with other churchgoers about how it was unacceptable to add or subtract from the Gospel, they would look at me like I was crazy — like I was some young kid who had recently experienced conversion and was now trying to preach to them.

"Come on," they would say, "we lived through the sixties and the seventies, and nobody believes this stuff anymore." They would add, "We believe a lot of what is preached to us, but at the same time, there's a lot we don't believe."

I would hear this and think, "Are these people serious?" The teachings of the Church are black-and-white. And I firmly believed that Catholicism required an all-or-nothing approach. It's not like going to a buffet where you take a little bit of this and a little bit of that, then reject what doesn't taste good to you.

The truth hurts sometimes. If we are going to be taught by God, the fisherman, we first need to be captured by Him. And His hook is going to have a bite. Of course, it's going to hurt. The truth hurts when we are sinners and when we acknowledge we are not surrendering to the truth.

And I didn't back down when it came to worrying if people were offended by the truth of the Church. I was pretty in-your-face about it all. Looking back, I was about as subtle as a bull in a china shop. If I saw a couple in church that had wedding rings on and no children, I would introduce myself and then say, "Isn't it terrible that people practice contraception? You two have kids, right?"

Almost inevitably, this would get them ticked off. They would look at me like, "Excuse me? Who are you?"

And then I would ask them point-blank: "Do you practice contraception?"

On one occasion, I caused such a scene that Father had to come over and separate me from a couple I had confronted.

It didn't take long before I became painfully aware that I was entering the Church at a time when many members were turning away from her teachings because the message is hard — especially in a secular and materialistic world where it is much easier for people to create their own personal Jesus. People aren't willing to accept objective moral truth, so they fall into moral relativism: "I wouldn't do it, but it's okay with me if you do." A more specific example would be, "I wouldn't have an abortion, but it's okay if you do."

Simply put, I was saddened by the things I was hearing from so-called Catholics. It almost made me want to cry. I began visiting various different parishes in different areas, figuring it might simply be the parish that was misguided. But everywhere I went I would see a lack of reverence at Mass. I would see and hear homilies that were absolutely dreadful and lacking in delivery. To me, it was clear that the world had gone astray because many of the people who God loves so much — people of His Church — had abandoned Him.

At the same time (though it pains me to say it), many of the priests I met were following the ways of the world, too. I got sassy with some of them sometimes and would say things like, "Why aren't you doing your job? You need to be preaching the truth from the pulpit." I was just so frustrated with hearing lame homilies, instead of hearing the call to deep conversion by adhering to all the teachings of the Church. Most of the homilies I heard sucked!

Sadly, I was equally concerned that some priests seemed to be living their vocation as if it were a career — like a 9-to-5 job — instead of offering their lives for souls. So many of the priests I met did not even wear their collar. They often dressed like a layman, so how was anyone going to know they were a priest? Policemen and firemen and nurses and doctors all wear uniforms, so you know who to go to when you need help. I felt like it should be the same for priests.

This explains why I found myself asking, "God, what have you brought me into?" I knew He had brought me into *the* Church that was definitely the bulwark of the truth, but I saw dysfunctional and incompetent members all over the place — members of the Church promoting women's ordination, homosexuality, contraception, etc. It sickened me.

Naturally, I shared my concerns with the priest at the Immaculate Conception Chapel, and he acknowledged that we were living in very difficult times. But at the same time, he encouraged me, saying that if you believe, you have to persevere. Just because they aren't living the message doesn't mean you shouldn't go through with it. That was great advice, and my prayer became, "Jesus, I trust in You!"

Ultimately, he and I agreed that we would meet one-on-one to go over basic concepts and to go through the doctrines of the Church. I emphasized to him, "This is what I want. I want meat; I want substance. I want the stuff that the saints, my brothers and sisters, were willing to die for. I've been to enough affirmation workshops. I want to know the truth!"

I became totally passionate about truth and started consuming books that would give me the meat, that substance I was looking for. But beyond the books and the words, I continued to lay myself bare at the feet of Mary. I would pray, "Mary, I love you so much and I am so in love with Jesus. I am so grateful for what you have given me. You are the Mother of God. You know Jesus. He is God, and you are His mother. And I believe that of all people you know Him best.

"Please cover me with your maternal mantle, for I am not the most brilliant man and could be easily deceived into believing or even making up my own Jesus. I want to know the real Jesus, the one whom so many people have turned away from. Without you, I am not going to know the real Jesus."

Mixed with my prayers was a sense of gratitude and humility. I know where I was when Mary found me and brought me to the feet of her Son, Jesus. I even said to Our Lady on one occasion: "Mother, you have called me to this and I know that it is because of you that I know the real Jesus. And I am totally willing to lay down my life and be a victim with Him because I should be dead. I don't deserve to live, yet I know that the fullness of truth has been revealed to me. So I accept it, and I am going through with my conversion to Catholicism."

During this entire period, my dad remained out at sea on the aircraft carrier. My mom was writing him letters, saying, "You are not going to believe the change that has come over Donnie." Being thousands of miles away, my dad was taking an "I'll believe it when I see it" attitude.

True to my intention, on the day he returned from sea, I was there to meet him at the dock. I embraced him and said, "Dad, I love you. ... Look at me. I am praying the Rosary. I go to church. I'm going to be confirmed and become Catholic."

Shortly afterwards, on my 20th birthday, June 29, 1992, the Calloways sat down for dinner as a family. Afterwards, as we cut into the big birthday cake my mom had made, I remember sitting across the dining room table from my father, mother, and brother Matthew when Mom asked me what it was I wanted for my birthday.

My response was unequivocal: "All I want is your forgiveness for everything I have done wrong," I began. "I am so sorry for everything I have done — all the ways I have hurt you and caused you such emotional pain. I need to have your forgiveness."

"Of course, you have it. Of course, you have our forgiveness," answered my mom without hesitation. Mom said she always saw the good in me, even when I was bad to the bone. And she knew things would eventually work out. She knew the power of God and knew that things like this could happen.

From that day forward, we were a Catholic family. Now we really knew each other. There were no masks and no shallow interactions. Now our relationship ran deep; I could pray with my family. And when you pray with someone, you are exposing them to one fundamental element — that is, you are not God. By getting on your knees and praying, it reveals how weak you are and how much you need God's help. Doing this as a family is extremely powerful. As a result of my conversion, I now have a love for my parents and brother that wouldn't have been possible without it.

Later that summer, I was finally confirmed at the Immaculate Conception Chapel. My entire family was there. I cried big time. My mother cried. Even the congregation cried as my father looked at me and said, "Welcome home, son."

He was right in more ways than one. For the first time in my life, I was indeed home.

13

POSTER CHILD FOR DIVINE MERCY

I'M SURE I STARTLED A LOT OF PEOPLE during my conversion period — especially all of my friends. Not surprisingly, my drug and drinking buddies didn't know what to make of the new me. Predictably, not to mention immediately, they began drifting away. One by one, they stopped calling. The reaction of these so-called friends was a real eye-opener. I came to the realization that if you took away the drugs and alcohol that brought us together, I had no relationship whatsoever with these people I called my friends.

But my former friends weren't the only ones who saw my behavior as radical. In the midst of my ongoing spiritual cleansing, I took virtually everything to the maximum. In those first days after my conversion, I spent each and every day in church praying all day long. I would go before the tabernacle and literally lie prostrate on the floor in front of Jesus. People would look down and assume that I had passed out, overcome by the intensity of my prayerful experience.

My radical ways even extended to my diet. I would fast or eat nothing but bread and water for three or four days at a time in an effort to go deeper. After I learned about the Stations of the Cross, I started praying them relentlessly — five or six times instead of just once. No one had told me you were only supposed to do it one time a day.

While some people believed I was going overboard, the Filipino ladies I had encountered on my very first visit to Our Lady of Victory appreciated my commitment and encouraged me. We soon became close friends. They would often remark, "It's so nice to see a young man who believes like you do." Throughout all of this, Fr. Callahan insisted on monitoring me for fear that I was a little too intense.

What my friends, Fr. Callahan, and these ladies didn't know was that I was spending a lot of time at Our Lady of Victory praying about how I could best serve God. I would kneel in church for hours asking what He expected from me. During this period, when I was attempting to discern God's calling for my life, one of these Filipino women approached me. She suggested that I pursue the priesthood. I was somewhat taken aback. I wasn't even Catholic yet, and this woman saw the priesthood in my future?

Shortly afterwards, she gave me several books. One was about the priesthood, while another contained postcards pre-addressed to a diverse array of religious communities. One could use the postcards to solicit information from the communities. I bought a roll of stamps and mailed in almost every postcard in the book. Sure enough, a handful wrote back to me.

In fact, the vocation director for one of these communities actually called me at home. It was a surreal conversation. I told him I was 20 years old and that I was very excited about the faith — that I loved Jesus and Mary and wanted to serve the Lord. Upon hearing this, he started to get very excited. I could almost hear him on the other end of the line thinking to himself, "Boy, this guy sounds like a really good candidate. He's the son of a military officer, a world traveler, and spends a lot of time in church."

"Tell me more," he urged. I went on to tell him how I had been homeless, in jail, in two rehab programs, and that I had done just about every illicit drug imaginable. And in the interest of full disclosure, I added, "Oh, and I'm not Catholic yet."

At that point, he cut me off and said, "I will pray for you, my son." Then he hung up on me. Was this payback for the time when I had hung up on a priest? I was extremely discouraged and confused by his reaction. On the one hand, my Filipino friends kept insisting I was destined to be a priest. Yet this vocation director's response suggested it might not be possible, not with a sordid past like mine.

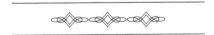

So, after receiving many like responses, I got confused. I didn't know where to turn. My mother saw all the mail I was receiving and would periodically ask how things were going. But I sensed she was hesitant to add her input. Maybe she felt I was in God's hands now. Or maybe she was still in shock over the fact that I was interested in the priesthood and religious life. The idea that I was going to take vows of chastity, poverty, and obedience and live in a community must have been startling.

Meanwhile, I didn't have a lot of patience in regards to

finding a direction. I was so zealous that I would have been happy going door-to-door with my backpack, crucifix, Bible, and rosary, telling people about Jesus and Mary.

Ultimately, I turned to Mary for guidance. I asked Our Lady, "Please guide me in this because I don't know what to do. I am so in love with you because you have shown me Jesus, but I can't serve Him without you. It has to be everything through you to sustain me and keep me on the right track. So I will reply to those communities that have your name in their title."

Naturally, there were quite a number of religious orders with Mary in their title. And after I responded to all of them, I received additional information from literally dozens of different communities.

I was still confused, so again I prayed to Our Lady, asking, "Guide me to the community you want me to visit and look into."

Trying to narrow down the possibilities, I told Mary I would proceed by only continuing correspondence with every community that used her name twice in its own name.

As I was culling my list, I came upon one community called the Congregation of Marians of the Immaculate Conception of the Most Blessed Virgin Mary. "Wow, this one referred to Mary *three* times," I thought. "This must be the one I am expected to focus on." Mary had not only answered my prayer, but she had, in effect, upped it one.

It wasn't long before I called the Marians and immediately had a good feeling about them. I spoke with the Vocation Director, Fr. Larry Dunn, MIC. Warm and friendly, he was open to visiting me at my parents' home in Norfolk, Virginia. Father Dunn had been in the Navy when he was younger and was excited that I lived on a naval base and that my father was a military officer.

When we discussed my recent conversion, his response was much more upbeat than the previous priests I had spoken with. "God is doing amazing things through Mary these days," he said. "Let's see what happens."

A few weeks later, Fr. Dunn spent the day visiting me and my family. My mom fixed a big Italian dinner, and everything she did and said made me look good. Beaming the entire time Fr. Dunn was in our presence, Mom was happy but also clearly relieved about the direction I was headed.

Afterwards, Fr. Dunn invited me to spend a weekend with the Marians in Washington, D.C. It would be the next step in the process of figuring out if we were a good fit for each other. When I boarded the Greyhound bus to Washington, D.C., I had no idea what to expect, but I was hopeful.

When I arrived at the Marian House, everything felt so right. It was peaceful and so filled with Mary's presence that I felt at home. The Marians are also the official promoters of the authentic Divine Mercy message and devotion. That, too, felt like a good fit for me. If anyone had experienced God's forgiveness, it was me. I had a front row seat. I considered myself a poster child for Divine Mercy.

I had come to know that The Divine Mercy message and devotion were one of the greatest gifts that God had given to the Church in our times. I had fallen in love with this message and the great secretary of God's mercy, St. Faustina Kowalska. At the core of this message and devotion is a spirituality of trust. As many people know, at the bottom of the image that depicts Jesus as The Divine Mercy is the inscription "Jesus, I trust in You!" It is precisely that spirituality of trust that I had welcomed into my life and wanted to tell others about.

So when I found out that the Marians were like *the* guys on the front lines when it came to spreading this message, I so wanted to be a part of that. As a matter of fact, Pope John Paul II even told the Marians in 1993 that they were to be apostles of Divine Mercy under the maternal mantle of Mary. What more could I ask for than being a Divine Mercy priest!

But what also excited me was that the Marians were orthodox and faithful. They clearly loved the Eucharist, the Pope, and observed the teachings of the Church. There were also young men there who were on fire and talked of Marian apparitions. They spoke about all the things that were really important to me and had brought me to Christ and the Church.

As the weekend came to a close, I was so enthused about what I saw and heard that I told Fr. Dunn I wanted to stay.

I didn't even need to return to Virginia; I offered to have my stuff shipped up to Washington, D.C. Father Dunn appreciated my enthusiasm, but he chuckled and said, "There's a little more involved to this process than that. Why don't you go home and pray about it. Then, if you decide to apply to our community, I will send you an application and we will begin the process."

When I went back home, I began praying. I felt an emptiness about not being with the Marians, which indicated to me that this was where God was calling me. I wanted to bear Mary's name, and this was the perfect opportunity.

Meanwhile, the Marians were honest and up-front about my prospects for acceptance. "You have a past-and-a-half," said the Washington house superior, "but if God is calling you to our community, we don't want to get in the way. We want to be open to God's will."

However, I learned that the application process wasn't the only obstacle I had to overcome. Becoming a priest is typically a long process, and it would be even more protracted for me. Normally, it takes approximately six years to become a priest, but in the event I was accepted, I would have an extremely long formation. For me, it would take about a decade — owing to the fact that I not only lacked a college degree, I didn't even have a high-school diploma.

I was only 20 years old, so at the time, a decade amounted to half my life. Yet, while the time commitment seemed daunting, I felt like I had nothing to lose. In my mind, I felt like I should have been dead already. Now I was getting a second chance.

"Don't get discouraged thinking about the length of time," counseled the house superior in Washington. "Always keep in mind that wine that ages over time is better." If that were the case, I would be like a very fine wine because the long journey towards priesthood would assure I was going to age for a long, long time.

I formally applied to the Marians in early 1993. Next came the formal application process, which proved difficult. Because of my background, remembering, reviewing, and explaining my past was trickier for me than for most applicants.

Like any other prospective candidate, I had to fill out a form that covered my family history and education, plus I had to provide my confirmation certificate, my baptism certificate, and all my high school transcripts. I also had to deliver seven reference letters and undergo a daylong psychological exam — one that involved answering an awful lot of inkblot questions. Finally, I had to write a five-page autobiographical essay and submit to a comprehensive medical exam.

After doing all of this, all I had to do was wait for an answer from the provincial superior and his four provincial councilors. Patience wasn't yet one my virtues, so the waiting for an answer was agony.

When Fr. Dunn called and notified me that I had been accepted into postulancy — the first year of formation — I was ecstatic. My mother was equally thrilled. At that point, I had been Catholic for almost a year, yet the Marians still decided to accept me and give me a chance. It was amazing that I was actually going to do this and, in a sense, live like they did in the early Church, where everything was going to be about Jesus and Mary and striving to save souls. Miracle after miracle was happening, and everything I had hoped for was coming true.

14

SPIRITUAL BOOT CAMP

ENTERING POSTULANCY IN THE LATE SUMMER of 1993 was a bittersweet time for me. Although it seemed like all my dreams were coming true, leaving my brother Matthew was painful for me. He had just turned 10 years old, and there was a part of me that wanted to stay and watch him grow up. Up until that point, I had been such a washout as a brother that I really wanted to make up for lost time. For the first time, I wanted to be a good example for him.

Making the break with him was even more difficult than I expected. When I boarded the plane for Washington, D.C., I actually broke down and cried. I couldn't come to grips with the fact that we would be living far away from each other, at least for the foreseeable future. But I knew that I was called to the priesthood, so God in His love for Matthew and me would bless and help both of us. I had faith that God would bring good out of our separation.

When I arrived in Washington, I moved into the Marian House with my fellow postulants. Yet I had one more spiritual detour to take before formally beginning postulancy. In 1993, Pope John Paul II was scheduled to appear at World Youth Day in Denver, Colorado. Through the Marians, I had the opportunity to attend. Of course, I jumped at the chance.

At the time, the Marians had a parish in Greensboro, North Carolina. So I made the five and-a-half-hour drive down with my fellow Marians. From there, we took a bus all the way to Denver — 1,600 miles and another 35 hours on the road.

The entire experience was so joyous. I couldn't believe it. Just one year after my conversion, I was going to be in the presence of the Pope. When he flew into Mile High Stadium in a helicopter, I was literally shaking with emotion, and my heart was beating out of my chest. This was my *father*. Adding to the excitement was the fact that this was the first time I had encountered other young Catholics who had such enthusiasm and passion for their faith. Afterwards, I couldn't wait to get back to Washington to begin my journey towards the priesthood.

What I discovered, though, is that postulancy felt a lot like starting over — especially from an educational perspective. Having been introduced to Marian community life, the local and very ordinary community college was quite a different experience. With only a GED to my credit, I essentially knew nothing about math, history, or science. As a result, I was required to attend community college for an entire year on my own dime. This amounted to 4,000 dollars, which I had saved through my job at the recreation center.

During postulancy, I lived with the Marians, studying the *Catechism of the Catholic Church* and attending daily Mass. But I inevitably had to spend long hours at school. And just like high school, my experience at community college was largely a miserable one.

For one thing, I struggled with completing the academic requirements. Even before I could take classes for credit, I had to complete basic courses in English and math. Learning fractions and other mathematical concepts was a painful struggle for me. I recall many a time when I ventured into the gym for the sole purpose of venting my frustrations on an available punching bag.

But even though I was frustrated, I remained cognizant of the fact that these basic requirements were required for me to achieve my goal. I willed myself to focus on studying unappealing subjects like math and history, even while I longed to be reading philosophy and theology. Again, I was learning the hard way that patience is a virtue.

Even more unsettling than the subjects I was studying was the environment at the community college. I was presented with a strange assortment of professors and fellow students that often had me questioning what I was doing in such a place. Many of the teachers encouraged what I viewed as immoral and blasphemous behavior. Needless to say, I was highly motivated to finish my basic requirements as quickly as possible.

After my year of postulancy, I entered novitiate — a kind of spiritual boot camp where you basically live like a monk for a year. During the novitiate, novices are under the guidance of a novice master, a priest on whom you must totally rely. You are required to maintain a very strict schedule from sunrise to curfew — one that dictates everything about when you study, pray, eat, and work.

As it happens, my novice master was hardcore. He was a former missionary. Being that he was accustomed to hunting wild animals for food and living without running water or indoor plumbing, he had no problem instilling discipline on myself and two fellow novices.

When I first met Fr. Gerry, I expected he would be impressed by the fact that I, too, was hardcore. I arrived at the National Shrine of The Divine Mercy in Stockbridge, Massachusetts (a small town in the western part of the state), for my yearlong stay with little more than what I could fit in a small backpack. Naturally, when I met Fr. Gerry, I expected he would be pleased with my minimalist approach.

"I'm ready. All I have is my backpack," I said, when introducing myself. He was unaffected.

"I'm going to test your mettle," he responded.

"What?" I had no idea what the word "mettle" meant. The only metal I knew about was heavy metal. I had to go look up the word in the dictionary. When I learned he was going to put my spirit, courage, and energy to the test, I got a little nervous. I wondered if he was going to try to break me before building me back up again — like they do in the military.

I soon learned I had no reason to be nervous. In fact, I found that I enjoyed my novitiate. Most men find it oppressive and count the days until it's over, but I loved the structure and discipline of it. I quickly adjusted to the routine and learned to appreciate the discipline it required. I needed it.

Our schedule went something like this: Every day we would get up early in the morning and eat breakfast with Fr. Gerry. Even though we all sat together at the same table, we weren't allowed to speak. That's because every night from 9 p.m. through the end of breakfast the next morning, we were subject to Grand Silence, which meant we had to remain silent. At first, I found it hard to keep my mouth shut 12 hours a day. But after I got accustomed to the silence, it came to seem natural. And believe me, it's powerful when you live in silence 12 hours a day for a year.

From 9 a.m. to noon, we would attend classes taught by Fr. Gerry, who would instruct us on prayer, the vows, and our community. We read encyclicals and all kinds of religious materials. Then, after lunch, we would all do work projects, normally manual labor like raking leaves or painting. Day in and day out, this was the routine.

In between, Fr. Gerry was very strict with us. We weren't allowed to watch television. We weren't allowed to use a computer. The Internet, if it had been widely available at the time, would have been off-limits. In our rooms, we could only have two books, a crucifix, a statue of Mary, and our clothes. As for bathing, we were limited as to how much water we could use — a clear indication of Fr. Gerry's missionary training — and were allowed just one clean towel per week.

In the very beginning, I had some difficulty adjusting to this routine because I was so impatient. As soon as we finished breakfast, I wanted to know the plan for the day. I would ask, "What are we doing today?" Father Gerry would refuse to tell me because he wanted me to surrender my will. At first, I would get all worked up about not knowing. But after a while, I began to realize that being obedient was peaceful. If you believe that God is working through your novice master, it makes life easy because you don't have to worry about anything. It becomes very freeing. But it took me a while to get into that mode.

Another thing I had difficulty adjusting to was the restrictions on eating. We were only allowed to eat three meals a day; no snacking allowed. We could eat a piece of fruit around 3 p.m., and that was it. Believe me, I ate that piece of fruit faithfully.

Father Gerry would always be keeping a close eye on portion sizes. At dinner, the tendency was to pile food on your plate, knowing that you wouldn't be eating anything for another 12 hours. But Fr. Gerry would watch and stop us novices from doing that. Admittedly, I would often be forced to take food off my plate. Although I grumbled about it at the time, Fr. Gerry's policy paid big dividends for me personally. The program put an abrupt end to my problem with night snacking, and I lost 30 pounds that year.

The overriding and most important lesson I learned during my novitiate was moderation. Coming in I was raw zeal. Not surprisingly, I employed and even insisted on an all-or-nothing approach.

When I first arrived in Stockbridge, I told Fr. Gerry I wanted to sleep just a few hours per night, so I could spend as much of my free time praying as humanly possible. "The saints didn't get eight hours of sleep per day," I would argue. Father Gerry opined that my intentions were noble, but that I wasn't an angel. He said, "If God calls you to be a saint, then fine. But right now I want you to get eight hours of sleep every night."

It was the same thing with driving. Whenever we got in a car together, I would want to drive as fast as the speed limit would allow and more. Father Gerry would say, "Don't go above 55 miles per hour." And then he would keep a close eye on the speedometer. It would drive me nuts. But after a while, I understood the lesson he was trying to teach me: moderation in all things.

As if that wasn't hard enough for my impatient spirit, Fr. Gerry also worked on my tendency to procrastinate and be lazy. I didn't understand the importance of attention to detail, and I would often try to get away with doing a job halfway. I had a hard time understanding that one of the greatest things you can do in the spiritual life is to be faithful to the little things, even if it's something as simple as raking leaves.

It's worth mentioning here that the Marians' property in Stockbridge, situated in the beautiful Berkshire mountains, is populated by hundreds upon hundreds of trees. Father Gerry had me spending many an afternoon raking leaves by hand — acres and acres of land. I broke many rakes — sometimes in frustration — before I came to the realization that raking leaves can be a perfectly valid way of loving and serving God. Sometimes, I wonder if all that raking wasn't payback for all the trees I cut down on my father's land in West Virginia.

After the novitiate year ended, I really came to understand how much I had become accustomed to the quiet and routine.

The day after novitiate ended, I ventured out to a mall to buy new clothes. It felt like I was going to a foreign country. There were so many unfamiliar noises, sights, and smells. My senses were bombarded, and I couldn't handle it. I felt like I was spiritually raped, and I wanted to retreat back into the novitiate.

So impressed was I by the entire experience that for a short time, I wanted nothing more than to become a novice master. In fact, I asked everyone in charge of me to train me for this future endeavor. I thought I was meant to instill the kind of spirit and discipline in men that I experienced. I even considered the possibility of taking things a step further and becoming a missionary like Fr. Gerry.

To test my conviction, I took a trip to Alaska in May and June of 2000. During my month in Alaska, I stayed in two different villages — Stebbins and St. Michael. These were Eskimo villages on the Bering Sea, both roughly 500 miles from the nearest paved road. The two villages are 10 or 15 miles apart. The only way to travel between them is to ride a four-wheeler with a shotgun on your back to protect you from bears and other wild animals.

While I loved the feeling of being in the middle of nowhere and appreciated the simplicity of the Eskimo lifestyle, it turned out to be far too radical for a lower-48 man like myself. To begin with, there was no running water and no indoor plumbing. I didn't eat much because the Yup'ik diet consists mostly of fish. I didn't sleep much because of the nearly perpetual daylight and because my living quarters were infested with all manner of creepy, crawling bugs. The villagers' hygiene was atrocious. Many villagers had hepatitis A because they used honey buckets (a five-gallon pail) as a communal toilet.

The most distressing part of the experience, however, was my up-close-and-personal experience with suicide, which is endemic among Alaskan Eskimos. Near the end of my stay, a teenaged girl blew her head off with a shotgun. I arrived at the scene about five minutes after the fact, and I saw her head splattered on the wall. "I am not ready to live so far from civilization," I said. So I high-tailed it back to Fairbanks.

Luckily, Our Lady agreed that I was not called to be a

missionary in Alaska. As I began to pray about my future, she made it clear that I was being prepared to be a different kind of missionary. And as I continued to pray, it became clear to me that I was being called to be a part of the new evangelization. My mission would be to rekindle a love for Jesus and Mary in the hearts of God's people. It would be a message of hope and a witness to mercy.

15

JOURNEY TO THE PRIESTHOOD

AFTER NOVITIATE, I MADE MY TEMPORARY VOWS of poverty, chastity, and obedience at the National Shrine of The Divine Mercy in Stockbridge, Massachusetts. Making my vows — on August 15, 1995 — was an amazing experience. It was somewhat ironic, too, because for most of my life, the last thing I had wanted was to be poor, chaste, and obedient. But there I was— with my parents and brother Matthew in attendance — totally surrendering myself to God and His Church. More than anything else, I wanted to enter into a covenant of love with God and live a radical way of life.

Shortly after making my first vows, I moved down to Washington, D.C., where I did another year at a community college. Then I enrolled at a Catholic university in the area to finish my undergraduate degree. After enduring a very difficult year at community college, I was overjoyed about the opportunity to finally study at a Catholic institution of higher learning. But it turned out to be a mixed blessing.

To be sure, this Catholic university's philosophy department was exceptionally strong, and I enjoyed studying philosophy. But the religious classes were a profound disappointment, as most were far too liberal for my taste. In fact, after completing the requirements for one class that I found particularly offensive — a class I like to refer to now as Heresy 101 — I literally burned my notebook. All that was left was the spiral binding. And that class was taught by a nun!

Meanwhile, resisting temptations of the flesh was equally challenging. The campus was populated by countless young, attractive women, and since I wasn't yet wearing clerical garb, the girls were flirting with me left and right. In fact, some of the young women continued to hit on me even *after* they found out I was preparing for the priesthood. Believe it or not, a few pursued me more aggressively than ever before. Perhaps they viewed me as a challenge. Or perhaps my commitment to becoming a priest made me seem like a "good guy," one who might make a good husband if I ever left the religious life.

I never gave in to temptation, but it wasn't easy. Just as I persevered in completing the required community college classes a year earlier, I persevered in my efforts to become a priest. As a safety measure to keep me away from the pretty girls, I grew a very long beard that would make any girl not even take a second look at me. I maintained that no temptation of the flesh would be strong enough to lead me astray. And no academic challenge would stop me from achieving my goal. By now, I was certain that I was called to the priesthood.

As divine providence would have it, after just one year at this university, my provincial superior asked me to be part of a group of four men charged with starting a new Marian House in Steubenville, Ohio — a city of almost 20,000 people situated on the banks of the Ohio River, an hour west of Pittsburgh. I jumped at the chance, because it afforded me the opportunity to enroll at Franciscan University of Steubenville. It's a Catholic school where the teachers take an oath of fidelity to the Pope and Magisterium, and the zeal on campus is phenomenal. I had so longed to be in a passionately Catholic academic environment, and I felt so blest to be moving to Steubenville.

A big reason why Franciscan University is such a special place is due to the inspired leadership of Fr. Michael Scanlan, TOR. I had attended a few summer conferences at Franciscan University and heard him speak. I was very inspired and impressed with how one man can make such a difference in the world.

Another big name at Franciscan University is Dr. Scott Hahn, whom I regard as being one of the best teachers I have ever had. During my two years at the university, I literally took every class Hahn taught. I would literally wait outside of the Registrars' office for hours, making sure I was the first one in line when registration began, so that I could get a seat in his classes.

I don't think I can adequately explain how powerful Hahn's classes are and how much they have influenced me. Some have said that attending Hahn's lectures is akin to trying to take a sip of water from a fire hydrant. His style of teaching is dynamic and powerful. It makes you want to love God with passion! I didn't even try to take notes in any of his classes. I would simply put my pen down, sit back, and enjoy basking in the goodness of a man on fire with the love of God.

In fact, after I graduated from Franciscan University in 1999 with a double-major in philosophy and theology, I wrote Dr. Hahn a note and slipped it under his office door. It read: "Dr. Hahn, I cannot tell you how much you have done for me. You have helped me so much to understand how God is my Father and I am His son, and how this relationship is a filial covenant. You will never know how much you have helped me to fall in love with my God!"

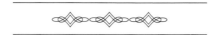

By the time I finished my studies at Franciscan University, I had already come a long way. This former high-school dropout now had a college degree from one of the best Catholic universities in the world — a development that no one appreciated more than my mom, dad, and brother, who were all on hand at my graduation ceremony. We all had tears in our eyes as we gathered together after I received my diploma. On a certain level, it was still difficult for all of us — including me — to comprehend that I had actually earned a college degree. Yet as far as I had come — and as proud as my family was — I still had a long way to go if I wanted to be a priest.

My next step was to return to Washington, D.C., to go to seminary, and attend the Dominican House of Studies, where I immersed myself in yet another academic program — a program that normally takes four years to complete. In keeping with my full-throttle mentality, I took it upon myself to take six or seven classes each semester. They included language courses in Greek and Latin, subjects that I never imagined myself studying. So in just three years, I graduated *magna cum laude* with a Masters in Divinity (M Div.) and an ecclesiastical STB degree, a bachelors in sacred theology granted only by Pontifical schools, which are recognized by the Vatican.

In the meantime, I continued to renew my vows every year, as temporary vows must be renewed every year for a minimum of three years. Finally, after being in vows for five years,

I petitioned to make my final vows of poverty, chastity, and obedience. After being accepted, I made my perpetual vows on March 25, 2000, at the National Shrine in Stockbridge, which meant that I was now a permanent member of the Marian community.

Even before I graduated from the Dominican House of Studies, I had already made the decision to continue my academic studies. Due to my intense love of the Blessed Virgin Mary, I wanted to try and find out as much about her as I could. I had Dr. Mark Miravalle as a teacher during my years at Franciscan University, and he was very inspiring in his love for Our Lady. So after Franciscan University, I had been doing my own research in all things Marian even while in seminary, but I wanted to somehow acquire a degree with a specialization in Marian Studies. At the time, I wasn't even sure if there was any place that offered such a degree. But I soon found out there was a place in Rome called the Marianum. Due to circumstances, I was not able to go to Rome to study. But I was overjoyed when I found out that they had a branch of the Marianum in Dayton, Ohio. It is called the International Marian Research Institute.

With the permission of my superiors, I applied to the International Marian Research Institute to begin studying for an STL in Mariology. An STL is an ecclesiastical graduate degree that requires rigorous academic work and the writing of a major thesis. It would require three summers of work to complete, plus about a year to write my thesis. As was the case at Franciscan University and the Dominican House of Studies, I became totally preoccupied with my studies.

Of course, it was easy to immerse myself in all things Mary at a place like the Institute, which features the world's largest collection of printed materials on the Blessed Virgin. I even had the chance to take classes from leading authors in Mariology like Fr. Luigi Gambero. I also had long conversations with Fr. Eamon Carroll, a world-renowned theologian and professor of

Mariology, who — I am sad to report — passed away in November 2008 at the age of 87. Perhaps most notably, I also had the opportunity to take the last class that Fr. René Laurentin taught at the Institute. For those of you not familiar with him, Fr. Laurentin has been one of the leading Mariologists for the past 50 years.

During the three summers I spent studying in Dayton, my love for Mary grew deeper and deeper. I even learned how to sing songs — in Latin — to Our Lady. But needing 20 credits per each six-week semester — and 60 credits overall — the academic workload was heavy. I would go to class six hours per day and then spend another six hours or so in the library — reading, researching, and writing until 1 a.m. On a typical night, I would sleep only four or five hours.

In hindsight, I can see that the rigors of the program took its toll on my body. During my first semester in Dayton, I developed a kidney stone, one of the most physically painful ailments I've ever endured. But even a kidney stone didn't deter me from studying day and night to learn as much as I could about Our Lady.

Naturally, at the tail end of the program, I had to write and defend my thesis before being awarded the degree. My thesis focused on St. Faustina Kowalska (1905-1938), the secretary of Divine Mercy who recorded in the *Diary of St. Maria Faustina Kowalska: Divine Mercy in My Soul* all the messages that Jesus and Mary wanted the world to know about God's greatest attribute. As you may know, St. Faustina was very Marian, and I chose to focus my research on the Marian element of St. Faustina's spirituality. Among other things, my thesis discussed St. Faustina's understanding of Mary's virginity, motherhood, mediation, and Mary being the Immaculate Conception. It also examined Faustina's personal relationship with Mary and the kind of imagery she used when talking about Our Lady.

My thesis took over a year to write. In its final form, it was over 200 pages long and contained more than 700 footnotes in Latin, French, Polish, Italian, and Spanish. Once the written version of my work was approved, I had to defend it — for an hour — in front of three priests. And keep in mind that all of them were — and are — doctors in the field of Mariology. Needless to say, I was a little nervous.

After working on my thesis for a year, I certainly knew my material, but the panel was what I would describe as "intellectually huge." I was confident in my ability to answer questions regarding most everything in my thesis, including the devotional aspects of Polish culture. But I wasn't nearly as comfortable putting everything in historical context. In the end, though, I must have acquitted myself well because I was awarded my STL *summa cum laude*.

In the years since completing my STL, I have found it to be both a practical and spiritual blessing. From a practical perspective, I now author books on the subject of Mariology and have a certain amount of intellectual credibility to back up my words. In fact, in 2008, Marian Press published a condensed version of my thesis in book form, which is titled *Purest of All Lilies: The Virgin Mary in the Spirituality of St. Faustina*.

Having an STL has also benefited me in my own spiritual life. After all, if you want to love somebody, you have to know them. And by getting to know all about Mary — all her titles and roles and who she is as a person — I have fallen even more in love with her and want to tell the whole world about her.

Early on in the process of studying for my STL, I took another important step in my progression towards the priesthood. In September 2002, I was ordained a deacon at the Basilica of the National Shrine of the Immaculate Conception in Washington, D.C. That was a major turning point for me because after many years of study, I finally had the opportunity to preach. Being ordained a deacon also allowed me to begin conducting baptisms, weddings, and funerals. So I began doing just that on the weekends at a parish in Maryland, while at the same time continuing to finish my seminary studies. Further, to my great joy, I was permitted to wear a Roman collar and a cassock — that distinctive long black robe that deacons and priests wear.

Meanwhile, back at seminary, I continued taking classes that taught me how to perform the duties of a priest — saying Mass, delivering homilies, hearing confessions, and the like. Naturally, though, when seminarians are learning how to say Mass in preparation for when they are ordained and are really doing it, plenty of mistakes are made. And not only were we asked to critique each other in class, all of our "dry Masses" were videotaped for the purpose of reviewing our own performances after-the-fact. The first few times I watched myself saying Mass, I practically had to avert my eyes. "Oh, my gosh! I look like that?" I cried.

The classes on how to give homilies were interesting, too. Personally, I had no problem with getting up and speaking in front of my classmates. The challenge for me — as for all my fellow seminarians — was to learn how to communicate in a way that would be viewed as open and friendly, while also coming across in an authoritative manner. Initially, it was torture for me to watch the video recordings of my homilies. I thought I was being so dynamic, only to discover — to my horror — that I looked like a robot.

In an effort to improve, I began scrutinizing videos of the renowned theologian Fulton Sheen (1895-1979). They were mostly old episodes of his television programs *Life is Worth Living* (1951-57) and *The Fulton Sheen Program* (1961-68) — both of which featured him speaking to a live audience. Watching Sheen, a master of public speaking, really helped me learn how to preach, using voice pitch, tone, and bodily gestures.

To this day, I almost never deliver a homily in which I work from a script. In my mind, it's of paramount importance for a priest to be passionate and romance the people from the heart. Even as far back as seminary, one might say that I already had a well-defined approach toward homilies. Instead of writing down my ideas, I focused my time on getting to know what Jesus and Mary wanted me to say to the people.

As one might expect, after six months of serving as a deacon in Maryland, I felt more than ready to be ordained to the priesthood. Generally speaking, a seminarian serves as a deacon for a minimum of six months before being ordained a priest.

Ultimately, I spent nine months as a deacon before finally being ordained a priest on May 31, 2003. It is a day I will never forget, even if the details are something of a blur. I recall experiencing a feeling of disbelief that after a 10-year journey, I was finally being ordained a Catholic priest. If only my old friends could see me now, I kept thinking. All the people from my past who thought I would always be a bum and would never amount to anything — I wished they could see me while the bishop was laying his hands on me and ordaining me to the priesthood. Even as he did, I remember his vestment of Our Lady of Guadalupe staring me in the face. Mary was with me.

After the ceremony, I was almost in a state of shock because I knew that I was changed. I would now be known as "Father Calloway." I now had the power to say, "I absolve you," to sinners in the confessional. I now had the power from God to change bread into the Body of Christ. Suddenly, I was acutely aware that I had reached a point where there was no turning back.

Not that I had any intention of turning back, of course. In fact, I could barely contain myself from going full-speed ahead. It's perhaps not surprising that at the reception following my ordination, I started preaching. As a matter of fact, one person in attendance described me as "bottled thunder." I had waited a decade to begin preaching and simply couldn't wait to mount the pulpit as a priest. "Stand back, here I come," pretty much describes the way I felt after I was ordained.

My first assignment as a priest was to serve as the assistant rector at the National Shrine of The Divine Mercy in Stockbridge. It was an awe-inspiring experience to have the opportunity to give spiritual direction — to say Mass, hear confessions, and preach about Divine Mercy and Our Lady. That first year I was a preaching machine. As promised, I spoke the *truth*, which made a lot of people in Stockbridge very happy, and as expected, also got quite a few liberal New Englanders upset. I'm still not afraid to offend anybody. I've learned to communicate the message with great love and mercy now, but I still don't water it down. Truth is truth, and I call a spade a spade.

Even from the earliest days of my priesthood, I was cognizant of the fact that not everyone wants to hear the truth. So, when you are speaking to large and diverse audiences, there are bound to be a few individuals who don't appreciate a black-and-white stance on issues like abortion, contraception and homosexuality. In fact, I've had people stand up in the middle of one of my homilies and begin yelling at me in front of the entire congregation.

On one particularly memorable occasion, I even had a 50-something woman rush up to me after Mass and take a swing at me. *She actually tried to punch me in the face.* I recall that my homily that day concerned New Age junk like horoscopes, reiki, and ouiji boards. Apparently, this woman had a son who took great interest in such things. After flailing away at me, she shouted: "The Jesus who I know is the Jesus who accepts people. He's tolerant and open minded."

I calmly responded: "Then you don't know the real Jesus. That's not Jesus. That's the one you've conceived in your mind to deal with your experiences in life."

Luckily, a couple of parishioners — who were both alarmed and shocked by her outburst — came between us and prevented her from continuing her assault. Once the parishioners ascertained the nature of her complaint, they came to my defense. In no uncertain terms, they advised this very angry woman that she didn't know what she was talking about and impressed upon her that the world needs more priests who speak the truth. We need priests, they told her, who don't hesitate to plant the hook of truth in the soul, even if it isn't exactly what a person wants to hear. Of course, the parishioners siding with me didn't placate her one bit. She was so ticked off that she stormed away in disgust.

Needless to say, incidents like this one haven't dissuaded me from speaking the truth. Not one bit. I recall one time when I went to preach at a Catholic high school in the Caribbean. When I arrived, I noticed a huge billboard on the grounds of the school promoting the use of condoms. The tag line of the ad read, "Pregnancy: Your decision."

When I spied the billboard, I turned to the people who invited me. I asked them, "This is a Catholic school, correct?" When they answered in the affirmative, I demanded to see the principal. My handlers started to freak out, thinking that I was going to go all John the Baptist on him — and I did.

To make a long story short, I went head-to-head with the principal, and he literally told me to leave the island. I was scheduled to address some of the classes that day as a visiting priest, but I never got the chance. But in the end, the principal repented. Within a few weeks, he had the billboard taken down and ultimately went to the bishop and apologized for the billboard *and* his behavior. Coincidence or not, he passed away less than a year later.

Sadly, though, it's priests who often take most offense when I preach. Not the majority of priests, of course, only the relatively small number who feel threatened by me calling them out of their comfort zone, the ones who see the priesthood as a career and not a call.

In my opinion, all priests need to strive for holiness and need to have a prayer life that is above average. Above all else, they need to have — without exception — the Virgin Mary in their life. When a priest has a woman in his life — Our Lady — it not only positively impacts his emotional and affective life, it affects the way he interacts with people. It helps him to be a gentlemen — to be gentle but also to be a man. Then, when there is a fight to be fought, he will fight off the wolves because he knows he's got a beauty that is worth defending.

I believe that a priest who doesn't have the Virgin Mary in his life is headed for big trouble because he's capable of doing a lot of damage to souls. Why? Because he is likely to have a wrong understanding of the Church since Mary is the one who teaches us how to truly love Jesus and His Church, which means a loving obedience to the teachings of the Vicar of Christ, the Pope. A priest who doesn't love Mary might sadly understand the Church only an as institution and start arguing that many of the moral teachings of the Church can change and should. It's only when he understands the Church as a loving mother who has the role to feed, nourish, teach, and admonish her children that he will be able to communicate that gift to others through his sacrificial love and obedience. No soul ever becomes holy without Mary, especially a priest.

As for my own priesthood, I had been ordained for a mere 10 months when my provincial superior called me into his office out of the blue one day. He said, "I have a proposition for you. I need a position filled — it's in another state. Would you be willing to fill it?"

Not knowing where he was going with this, I responded, "What's the position?"

He went on to ask: "Are you willing to move to Ohio and become house superior at our Marian House of Studies in Steubenville?"

My first reaction was, "Like, yeah!," but not so much because I wanted to be a house superior, but because I loved Steubenville. Plus, my parents and my brother Matthew lived just three hours away. It seemed to be the perfect situation.

As it turned out, my experience in Steubenville exceeded my lofty expectations. Not only did I thrive in my role as house superior, within months I was named co-vocation director for the Marians. Then, less than a year after that, I became the sole vocation director — entrusted with recruiting new men to our community. And I simply love this role that has been entrusted to me and hope to do it for years to come. I want to raise an army of good, holy priests for Jesus and Mary.

What does being a vocation director entail you might ask? In part, it involves coordinating monthly retreat weekends at the Marian House in Steubenville, where interested young men visit. Over the weekend, I give talks about what it means to be a priest, what it *doesn't* mean to be a priest, and all the things that are necessary to become a priest. I tell these men that you have to love the Church and accept all of its teachings. I communicate the practical realities of making vows of poverty, chastity, and obedience. Of course, I talk to them about the Marians in particular — all of our ministries, where we live, and exactly what it is we do.

Then, if an individual is interested in applying to our community, I help him through the application process. I'm responsible for collecting all the information necessary to complete the individual's application — academic transcripts, birth certificate, baptismal certificate, reference letters, an autobiographical essay, among other things. Once all the reports are in and the information is compiled, I write up a presentation for the provincial superior. And if the provincial says "yes" and a candidate is accepted, I hand him off to the Marians' postulant director.

As vocation director, what I've found is that the vast majority of men that I talk to about the possibility of pursuing religious life have had their share of struggles in life. Most of them have been born Catholic, but they either left the faith or didn't fully grasp it, or were lukewarm and became dead in their faith. Many attended Catholic colleges at one time or another, but they lost their faith after being taught by Sr. Social Justice and spending all of their time partying and chasing girls.

Yet, at some point they had a conversion experience. Personally, I love that. These men come in with a fresh approach and such zeal, sick of the ways of the world and all it offers. They are often referred to as being part of the JP II generation, because many of them discerned their vocation during the pontificate of John Paul II. Although I didn't know about JP II during my "crazy years," during my 10 years of studying for the priesthood, I looked to him as a model of what it meant to be a priest. So do the guys who are joining now. They want exactly the same things — love for the Blessed Virgin Mary, zeal for proclaiming Divine Mercy, love for the Eucharist, faithfulness to the Church, and they have a burning desire to wear the collar out in public. They want to let people know they are there for them. Truth and mercy are what they are all about.

At the same time, it's important to recognize and understand that it's not necessarily easy for these individuals to make the transition to religious life. Eighty years ago, young men would begin the journey to the priesthood at a very young age, and the religious life was all they knew. Today, the men coming to community tend to be older — often in their late twenties or thirties. In many cases, they have had careers, owned their own cars, and even owned a home. They've been part of a culture that embraces radical individualism and consumerism. Giving all that up — when you've had it all along and it's all you've ever known — requires a certain amount of deprogramming. Candidates can't think of themselves anymore. They have to think of the community. And that can be a difficult adjustment.

What's interesting about this is that the conventional wisdom is that many men are dissuaded from becoming a priest because priests aren't allowed to marry. I haven't found this to be true. In fact, I haven't talked to one man discerning the priesthood who is uptight because priests can't marry. I find that what most men struggle with is the dying-to-self that is required when coming out of a culture where you can do whatever you want, whenever you want, with whomever you want. Transitioning from that to being obedient to a superior can be tough.

From a distance, the religious life probably seems somewhat romantic. But when you get in, you realize you have to strip yourself of all attachments, things you probably didn't even realize you were attached to. As a result, a certain percentage of men come in and quickly realize they can't do it.

Meanwhile, another interesting misconception concerns the so-called vocations crisis. From time to time, you'll hear or read a story in the media proclaiming that there is a grave shortage of young priests. I don't believe this is true either. In my mind, that is like saying there are no fish. There may be a *depletion* in the number of young priests, but as a vocation director, it's my job to go out into the world and be a fisher of men. Again, I'm not out there telling them the priesthood is a career or a job. It's a calling, and if you want to die for the love of your God and the good of souls, you will respond to it.

And you know what? The Marians are certainly not experiencing a vocations crisis. In the handful of years that I have been vocation director, we've attracted more than a dozen men who are now in various stages of the formation process. The response we've seen has been phenomenal. As a result, the future of our community looks awesome! A new generation of Divine Mercy priests is on the horizon.

For the benefit of those of you who might be interested in discerning a call to the priesthood, I'll briefly describe what is entailed in becoming a Marian priest. Essentially, the process remains the same as what I experienced — although men who already possess a college degree would have a shorter road to travel than I did. In a nutshell, the process goes something like this:

Once he is accepted by our provincial, a man enters postulancy, which normally lasts one year and generally takes place in Ohio. During this time, a postulant lives with the Marians at our house in Steubenville and experiences community life. At the same time, he takes classes at Franciscan University in philosophy and pre-theology.

After postulancy, he enters the novitiate for one year. In the novitiate, he learns about the history of spirituality and prayer, the vows, and the charism or main aims of our community. As I noted earlier, novitiate can be described as spiritual boot camp. Novices are assigned work projects during the day

— many of them solitary in nature — so it's a very introspective time. A man really gets to know himself and his own strengths and weaknesses. Essentially, novitiate lays the foundation for living the rest of one's spiritual life in a religious community.

Following novitiate, a candidate makes temporary vows of poverty, chastity, and obedience, which are renewed for a minimum of three years before there is the possibility of making permanent vows. During this time, a candidate continues his studies while in seminary (which typically lasts four years). Then he is ordained a deacon and gets some parish experience working with people. Finally, after serving as a deacon for six months to a year, he is ordained a priest and receives his pastoral assignment. A new Marian priest most likely serves in Stockbridge or at one of our parishes in the Midwest. But those who desire can continue their studies and get a doctorate. They can go to Rome, for example, or Poland for their doctoral studies. And for those who want to be missionaries, we have missions, including a brand-new mission in the Philippines.

All in all, we are always looking for a few good men.

16

ITINERANT
PREACHER

AS I SHARED EARLIER, there was a brief interval when I believed I was called to serve the Marians as a novice master. By the time I completed my own novitiate year, I had convinced myself that I had good qualities for the task — a good mix of discipline and zeal — to lead new members of our community through spiritual boot camp. I wanted to instill in novices the kind of spirit and discipline that Fr. Gerry had instilled in me over the course of our year together in Stockbridge. I even grew a very long beard and consciously took on the distinctive, unmistakable look of a monk in an effort to further the image I sought to project — that of a disciplined, rugged spiritual warrior.

But as I prayed about my future, I began to question whether Jesus and Mary wanted me to be a novice master. Our Lady, in particular, was speaking to my heart and telling me that my mission would not entail that aspect of forming men. As my Lady and Queen, she knows that I have a very knightly type of spirituality, one that seeks to win battles for her and exercise manly chivalry in defense of all that is good, true, and beautiful. So it was that Mary began communicating her desire for me to tell others what God — through her — had done for me and wanted to do for others. Namely, I was being called to share my conversion through Mary and Divine Mercy. Slowly, I was able to let go of my desire to be a novice master and came to the realization that I needed to do two things: To tell the world my conversion story and to go out to the whole world as an apostle of Divine Mercy.

At first, I wondered how I could possibly reach an audience so vast. You'll recall that my first assignment as a priest was as assistant rector at The National Shrine of The Divine Mercy in Stockbridge, where my day-to-day responsibilities didn't allow for many opportunities to travel. However, on one of the handful of trips I made during the first 12 months of my priesthood, I had the chance to make a pilgrimage to European Marian Shrines. During that trip, I met a man in the Frankfurt airport on his way to Medjugorje. He introduced himself and asked me about myself and what I was doing.

Needless to say, one thing led to another, and I ended up

telling him my conversion story. He found it absolutely amazing and said that people needed to hear it. And as divine providence would have it, he offered to record it and spread it!

To make a long story short, the video we produced soon circulated to the ends of the earth. As a result, I began to receive invitations to tell my conversion story all over the United States — and before long — all around the world. At first, I could only accept a handful of invites, owing to my responsibilities at the National Shrine. But over time, I was able to accept more and more speaking engagements — just as Our Lady planned. In fact, today one of the major aspects of my ministry is speaking to audiences the world over about Jesus and Mary.

And my speaking engagements just keep increasing. I might add that the offers to speak increased exponentially when the president of a very popular Catholic communications group in California offered to tape and market my conversion story with his company. As a result, I now get between three to five offers a week to speak. I have just been amazed at how Jesus and Mary have worked in my life!

Looking back, I find it difficult to believe that I once harbored thoughts of becoming a novice master, because that lifestyle is so at odds with the gypsy-like existence that I have always embraced. Certainly, if I served as a novice master, I would have nowhere near the same number of opportunities to travel and preach that I have today. And right now, I am so enthralled by serving as an itinerant preacher and recruiting men to the priesthood that I can't ever imagine doing anything else.

Serving as an itinerant preacher is hardly a new phenomenon. For one, St. Paul used to do it. He would be in one place for a short while. Then he would move on, planting seeds far and wide and stoking fires here, there, and everywhere. There seem to be more and more priests serving in this capacity today — with great effectiveness, I might add. I believe it's because there is such a great need for a new evangelization of God's people. Certainly, there is a need for missionary work in third world countries, but there are so many poorly formed Catholics that need to be evangelized just the same.

As I see it, part of my role is to provide people with the Gospel truth, so that their hearts are convicted of good and evil. Then I seek to give them a huge dose of Divine Mercy. When I give a presentation, I let my audience know who Jesus and Mary really are — to remind them why Jesus and Mary are so worthy of being loved. I talk to them about sin. Then I tell them about the love of God and urge them to fall in love with God, the Blessed Virgin Mary, and the Church. I also admonish them to go to confession. After all, it's free, and it's the one Sacrament you can go to 24/7. For those in the audience who are already in love with Jesus and Mary, I urge them to go deeper.

In some ways, I see myself as a Special-Forces-type-of-preacher. I'm always on the move, ready to swoop in and address a spiritual crisis before withdrawing and leaving my audience in the care of the local pastor.

In some ways, then, I am patterning my ministry after John Paul II. He was the most traveled Pope in history — in part because he took advantage of the speed and reach of modern transportation. Today, one can be halfway around the world in a matter of hours, and as you will soon see, I frequently find *myself* halfway around the world. Not that I have a problem with that. To the contrary, I love the idea of traveling and seeing new places and meeting new people. I also enjoy learning from the people I meet in the course of my spreading the truth of Catholicism.

In the course of my travels, I have met, and been in the presence of, some of the most remarkable people in the world. Prior to his death in 2005, I was in the presence of Pope John Paul II on several different occasions. The first time, it was in 1993 at World Youth Day in Denver. The second time was in 1997 in Rome, when John Paul II met with a group of young religious of which I was a part. Then I saw him again in Poland in 1999 when our two Marian martyrs (Blessed George Kaszyra, 1904-1943, and Blessed Anthony Leszczewicz, 1890-1943) were beatified in Warsaw and John Paul II blessed our Marian Shrine of Our Lady of Lichen, which happens to be the largest and second-most visited shrine in Poland. On that occasion, I was just five or six feet from John Paul II — absolutely in awe of the man. I never did get to shake his hand or touch him. But, still, being in his presence was a dream come true.

I was also super blessed to meet Mother Teresa of Calcutta on three separate occasions while she was visiting in Washington, D.C. On one occasion, I even had the opportunity to embrace her and hold her hand as she talked to a crowd of priests and nuns. That was amazing because I knew I was touching a saint. She is now Blessed Mother Teresa, so it's just a question of time before she is canonized.

Believe it or not, I've even had the chance to meet a few celebrities, including Mexican model/movie star/heartthrob Eduardo Verástegui (star of the movie *Bella*). He is a devout Catholic and renowned for using his high-profile celebrity status to advance Catholic truth. He approached me at a conference in California, told me he had seen my conversion video, and thanked me for doing it. Naturally, I don't keep up on celebrities. So, at the time, I didn't even realize who I was talking to. As soon as he walked away, my friends advised me I had just been complimented by Eduardo Verástegui. "*Eduardo Verástegui!* Don't you know who he is?" they cried. I had no idea at the time, but when I saw *Bella*, I was so grateful to have met him.

At the same time, my speaking engagements have also offered me the opportunity to visit some of the most amazing locales on the planet. For one, I don't think I've ever seen a more beautiful place than the South Island of New Zealand. It reminded me so much of *Lord of the Rings*. It also had a primeval feel to it. The entire time I was there, I expected a Pterodactyl to come flying at me.

I've also fallen in love with the Outer Hebrides and the highlands of Scotland, which I visited during a trip to the British Isles with my mother a few years back. There is something majestic and medieval about Scotland that really appeals to me.

And I certainly would be remiss if I didn't mention the islands of the Caribbean. My various trips to Grand Cayman have been unforgettable, especially snorkeling amongst barracudas and giant sea turtles. While I was there, I also ventured over to Stingray City, a series of shallow sandbars found in the North Sound of Grand Cayman where I swam with huge southern stingrays.

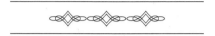

Of course, the joy I get when preaching to large audiences of souls is way more inspiring than any of the natural wonders I have seen. Sometimes I have to pinch myself to make sure I'm not in the midst of a dream. For instance, I once had the opportunity to speak at a Catholic conference at Notre Dame in South Bend, Indiana. Ten years earlier, no one would have ever dreamed I'd be telling my conversion story to thousands of people at Notre Dame University. Yet there I was, preaching to a huge throng of Catholics — rising up all around me in stadium seating. Thanks to the configuration of the seats, I was able to connect with the audience and feed off their energy in a way that wouldn't be possible in a typical parish church. I still vividly remember the moment when I paused to hold up the picture I brought with me where I have really long hair. The organizers projected that image onto the towering video screens in the arena, and the crowd *roared* in response. The audience was so responsive, so emotional, and so *loud* that I did some apostolic preaching that day!

If you're wondering what issues I cover when I give a presentation at a Catholic conference or other event, I usually begin by telling parts of my conversion story and relate my experiences of coming into the Church. This always seems to resonate with people, no matter what the occasion. Then I go on to discuss some of the changes the world and the Church have gone through in the past 40 or 50 years. I explain why so many Catholics are now practicing what many call "cafeteria Catholicism" — that is, accepting certain tenets of Catholicism while ignoring or rejecting others. Then I delve into what I refer to as the "hard" issues and preach the truth as it is given by the One, Holy, Catholic, and Apostolic Church.

I find that most listeners love and appreciate my no-nonsense style. It's almost as if they have been waiting for a priest to effect a come-out-swinging, take-no-prisoners approach. In fact, I've heard young men refer to my talks in terms of battle, as in, "Father Calloway presents the priesthood as if a priest is a warrior and somebody's attacking his bride!" That might be a somewhat militaristic way of describing what I do, but there's a certain degree of truth to it.

When you think about it, a priest is like Braveheart — the famous Scottish warrior who seeks to defend his people against the enemy. If you're a man and someone is beating up your bride and you sit back and watch her being beaten, then you are a failure. And that's what the Church is to a priest — a bride. A priest has to be willing to fight for the Church's honor and defend her with spiritual weapons. It goes without saying that I defend the Church with love and mercy and compassion, but I definitely draw a line in the sand.

Sometimes people have asked me if I ever get tired of telling my conversion story. The answer is a huge no. I love telling it because it is as though I get to praise Jesus and Mary all over again for what they have done for me. Sure, there are times when after giving my witness three or four nights in a row, I feel like I wrote the old Bob Seger song "Turn the Page." ("Here I am, on the road again. There I am, up on the stage. Here I go, playing the star again. There I go, turn the page.") I envision myself in a tour bus, going from city to city, repeating the same routine day after day. So just like anyone else, after a while, I need time off to decompress and recharge my batteries.

As I alluded to earlier, the spiritual needs of Catholics are so great these days that I have been bombarded with requests to speak at such things as youth events, schools, workshops, jails, prisons, rehab facilities, and the list goes on and on. And I love them all. Sometimes it's hard to balance it all, but somehow it all works out.

Not long ago, I spoke at the National Catholic Conference on Alcoholism in San Diego, where I related what I sometimes refer to as my "Divine Detox experience." I emphasized how prayer, humility, repentance, and devotions play a huge part in coming out of substance abuse. I've also visited a handful of drug rehabilitation-type facilities — typically to address a small group — where I like to think that my personal experiences give the addicted hope.

I have to admit, though, that speaking to individuals battling substance abuse is not the easiest thing for me to do. To this day, when I hear the words "small group," I immediately flash back to the counseling sessions I experienced during my youth and get a little bit panicky. But I'm willing to put myself out there and speak to these souls because I know it's a worthwhile endeavor. Anyway, when I'm leading a so-called small group, I'm assured the session won't devolve into singing corny songs and making s'mores, if you know what I mean.

Meanwhile, I've also been receiving more and more invitations from men's conferences these days. Personally, I think it's because so many men are being affected by the pornographic age in which we live. It means a lot to them when one of their own has not only struggled with these things but continues to be a work-in-progress, sharing insights with them on how to combat the wickedness of lust.

The experience of speaking at these conferences benefits me greatly. Although some individuals believe I am somehow above temptation, I am still enticed as much as any other man, particularly in regards to temptations of the flesh. So it's a little frustrating on those occasions when an individual approaches me after one of my talks and says, "I just wanted to touch you," while simultaneously giving me this look that says they believe I can do no wrong. Sometimes a person will even come right out and say, "You are so holy. You no longer suffer from temptation. You are a saint."

No, I tell that individual, pray for me because I am tempted, too — perhaps now more than ever. Let's face it: We're all living in a very sexual, visual culture that saturates our senses, thoughts, and memories. Most people can hardly go a day without being exposed to sexual content, whether it be in television commercials, music, movies, or magazines. And the Internet has only made the situation worse, because hardcore sexual imagery is now not only free, it's just a mouse click away.

But the comforting thing about a men's conference is that a man quickly comes to the realization that he is not alone. Believe me, the worst thing a man can do is struggle with temptation in isolation with no accountability; it's much easier to overcome your problems when surrounded by brothers who can empathize and provide support.

Finally, one last venue that I'd like to mention is the correctional institution. Over the years, I have spoken at a handful of prisons around the world, and it's never a comfortable experience. It's not because of the nature of the audience, but because making the arrangements and then clearing security always seems to be an arduous, invasive, time-intensive process. To perform a one-hour speaking engagement at a prison, I've found that I need to budget at least three hours to pass through security.

And believe it or not, sometimes the prison guards give me an extra hard time simply because I am a priest. It seems they have become so jaded that they automatically assume that everyone in prison is a liar, a thief, a manipulator, or a thug. They never seem willing to give prisoners the benefit of the doubt or the opportunity to change. Once, I even had a prison guard tell me off. He said, "You think these guys are going to change because you're a priest? — his voice taking on a condescending tone as he glanced at my collar. "One minute, the inmates will say, 'Glory to God.' And the next minute, they will stab you," he sneered.

All I could say was, "You may be right. But I've got to hold out hope. Because I've been through some of the same experiences they have, and my life has changed. And I know

I'm not the only one. And by the way you think, you're more a prisoner than they are." This particular guard didn't want to hear it. In fact, he deliberately made my security screening extra difficult. Sometimes, the guards are so hardened that I feel like a prison visit is more of a ministry to the guards than the prisoners.

Nevertheless, some of the most remarkable experiences I've ever had occurred at prisons. On one particularly memorable trip, I spoke at a maximum security facility in the Caribbean, inside a very institutional-looking beachfront fortress that featured a spectacular view of the ocean. I had to drive up a twisting, turning one-lane road to access the facility, which was encircled by a high barbed-wire fence and ringed with guard towers. The prison was dirty and smelly and the heat was suffocating, but the locale was paradise, provided you weren't locked inside, of course.

On this particular day, I spoke to upwards of 200 hardened criminals for two hours. To tell you the truth, it was quite intimidating. As I looked out at the audience, I saw men who had been imprisoned for crimes ranging from murder and kidnapping to drug trafficking and rape — men with scars on their faces and on their souls. It was a lot more frightening than speaking at a parish or at a youth conference. Sure, there were armed guards ready to come to my defense at a moment's notice, but many of the prisoners in this facility were serving life sentences and would have little or nothing to lose if they chose to assault me.

As soon as I began speaking, however, I relaxed, as my words seemed to resonate with the men in front of me. On this particular occasion, I emphasized my past struggles with substance abuse and peppered my language with the kind of slang terms that would authenticate me and prove that I could identify on some level with the challenges they had faced in their own lives. I went into the kind of graphic detail that would never be appropriate for a parish audience. I even showed the prisoners my Grateful Dead tattoo, which seemed to fascinate them and provide a sense of authenticity to my words. I believe it was because of my dark past that they could imagine me as "one of them." In fact, I'd like to think that my journey from total darkness to the priesthood gave them hope.

I'm pretty sure I had an impact because as soon as my talk was over a Columbian prisoner with very long hair approached me. He began speaking very fast — in Spanish — and as he spoke, tears welled up in his eyes. I understand some Spanish, but I couldn't comprehend what he was saying because he was speaking super fast. Fortunately, one of the visitors with me was able to translate for me. He said, "He's thanking you for your talk and telling you how grateful he is." Then he paused for a moment before adding: "And he says your Spanish was excellent."

Of course, I hadn't given my talk in Spanish — only in English. Yet somehow this particular individual had heard my talk in Spanish.

When the person translating advised him that I didn't speak Spanish, he completely lost it. He said, "My God, you let me hear it in Spanish?" as he looked to the heavens. This prisoner — who, it turns out, had committed multiple homicides as a cocaine runner and was now serving a life sentence — started crying his eyes out. He related how he had grown up Catholic but turned away from the Church years earlier. But when I flashed the picture of me with my long hair, he began to identify with my story.

In some ways, the reaction of this Colombian prisoner is not unlike that of other prisoners I've connected with. After I speak at a parish or a men's conference, the attendees typically stand and applaud. And that's wonderful, of course. Afterwards, there are always a handful of listeners who will approach me and thank me in person or relate a personal anecdote. But after a talk in prison, it's common for one or more of these muscle-bound, tattooed, convicted criminals to rush up to me and give me a bear hug. It's a little scary, but also it's pretty cool.

Interestingly, these men are often sincerely remorseful about the things they've done. They say things like, "Father, I'm here because I had one bad night. I was drunk and got into a bar fight and killed a man with a pool stick. I got carried away and one thing led to another and here I am for the next 25 years." Stories like these always make me stop and think, "That could have been me."

Another thing that's a little different about a visit to a prison (as compared to a parish or conference) is the message I deliver. For one, I invite the inmates to make the best of their situation, difficult though that may be. It goes without saying that prison — especially a maximum security facility — is not a happy place. Yet it's not entirely unfriendly to someone interested in living a religious life. It is very possible to have a conversion experience on the inside.

Allow me to explain. I often tell prisoners that if they are interested in having a conversion experience while in prison that can most readily occur by choosing to live like a monk. After all, monks live in places that are essentially locked down; they even refer to their living quarters as cells. So if a prisoner can adjust his outlook, he can undergo a conversion that makes him a better person. This explains why I urge inmates to strive to do more than simply exercise, lift weights, and tell war stories. It's very realistic to be transformed and become holy in a place that most people see as decidedly unholy. An inmate can become holy if he only allows himself to change for the better. And many, many prisoners have taken this advice to heart.

In fact, in some ways, the atmosphere of a prison may help men to discover God because prisoners are not able to do their own will. The essence of being a monk is to die to yourself and do the will of God through your superiors. So if a man can transform that into something religious, he can begin living a routine of discipline that could conceivably lead him to become a saint while in prison. It won't be easy, but prison is definitely conducive to a monastic existence.

The greatest challenges would be exhibiting patience and being merciful, because a prisoner probably isn't going to receive a lot of mercy from the guards. If a prisoner's language changes and he begins praying on a regular basis, the guards will probably start to psychoanalyze him. And that prisoner is also likely to be ridiculed and ostracized by other inmates. So a man looking to lead a religious life while in prison would have to be willing to carry a cross that is more confined. Out in the world, a man can always go back home, but in prison physical and emotional escape is obviously not possible. Fighting the temptation to be angry at being incarcerated and enduring the incarceration as part of your plan of growing in holiness would also present significant challenges.

Every so often, I am asked if there is a forum where I'd like to make a presentation but haven't yet had the chance. The answer is yes. If I had my druthers, I would absolutely love the opportunity to speak at a seminary. In my mind, there would be nothing more exciting than to address a large group of men preparing for the priesthood — to pump them up and implore them to be holy, zealous, and faithful.

Of course, I've had countless seminarians attend my talks over the years. I've noticed that they do respond differently to my message than laypeople. I think it's because they know they are going to be wearing a collar at some point and that people are going to be listening to them.

If I ever do get the chance to address a group of seminarians, I know exactly what I would say to them. I would acknowledge the importance of the academic aspects of their journey, but also emphasize that seminary is a time for them to grow in holiness. Seminaries are meant to be saint factories. It's a time to strive to be a saintly man — to take a strong papal, Eucharistic, and Marian dimension into one's spirituality. My final bit of advice? "Wear your collar and let people see you praying," I'd say.

Much in the same way that I'd like to speak at a seminary, there are still many places I'd like to visit to deliver God's message. Near the top of the list is Rwanda — a destination that is actually quite realistic, considering that Rwanda is home to an approved Marian apparition site (in Kibeho). Also, the Marians have a House there. I'd also love to do ministry and speak in American Samoa, which is an unincorporated territory of the United States.

As you may have noticed, though, neither Rwanda nor American Samoa are among the places that I terrorized during my youth. As it happens, I've already been back to preach at almost every place I lived in my "past life," with one very notable exception: Japan.

Whenever I return to one of these places — cities like Virginia Beach or San Diego, for instance — I like to think of it as a stop on a kind of "Reparation Tour." I treat it almost as if I'm going back and making up for what I did wrong by giving people hope and helping others to find the God of mercy. Also, the prior relationship helps people in these places to identify with my story, because their city is part of my story.

For example, when I went back to Hawaii for the first time to tell my conversion story in Honolulu, I opened by saying, "It's great to be back in Hawaii. The last time I was here I was in shackles and chains, being escorted through Honolulu International Airport by military police." Everyone's jaw dropped because they didn't yet know my story. But after they heard my witness, they went from being shocked by what I had done to identifying with me and taking a certain ownership of the Fr. Donald Calloway story.

It was a similar situation the first time I returned to New Orleans. I opened my talk with the line: "The last time I was in New Orleans, I got arrested for stealing a case of beer from a supermarket and got thrown in jail. I spent a very scary night in the slammer with five of the biggest, baddest dudes you'll ever see." Immediately, the audience began to identify with me because, in a certain sense, God was allowing New Orleans to be part of the story. I've had similar experiences in Virginia Beach, San Diego, Los Angeles, and a number of other different places. It's amazing how many people identify with my story, even those who come from different cultures. My story is so multicultural that almost everyone can relate in one way or another.

At the same time, it can also be a little bit therapeutic for me to return to certain places. For a long time, I had nothing but bad memories of New Orleans, so the thought of going back made me terrified. But when I finally worked up the courage to return, I met an awesome group of Catholics, and they made me feel so welcome. It was just another example of God's mercy and how stepping out in trust can truly work miracles and bring new life to a person.

I had similar feelings about San Diego as well. When I first returned after my conversion, I felt a certain angst because, for all intents and purposes, it was there where a lot of my youth rebellion really began. Now it's my favorite city in the entire country. If I could live anywhere in the U.S. again, it would be San Diego. There's a reason they call it "America's Finest City."

But the one place I haven't been able to speak in since my conversion is Japan. On various occasions, I've been able to fly through Tokyo's Narita International Airport for layovers while in route to Guam or the Philippines. But I have not had the chance to speak in Japan yet.

Naturally, I have made a big deal of my various layovers in Japan, telling everyone that I was finally going back to Japan. Most people immediately assumed I was going there for a speaking engagement. They wondered if I was afraid of encountering any trouble with the authorities. I tried to reassure them, saying, "I've got a new passport now. It's not like I'm a wanted man or anything."

Meanwhile, my mom was so happy for me, saying, "Isn't it neat after all that has taken place that you will now be going back, even if you are just passing through?" She hoped I'd have time to venture outside the airport and do some shopping and sightseeing.

As it turns out, I never ventured outside the terminal. But that didn't make the trip any less dramatic. Flying out of LAX, a lot of different emotions came rushing back. There was the memory of my very first flight to Tokyo: When I imagined that moving to Japan was all a bad dream and that when I woke up, I'd be on the beach in San Diego, primed to continue living the California dream. As soon as I got off the plane and walked into the terminal to catch my connecting flight, I had this profound

"I'm back" kind of moment. The sights and smells and sounds and the way everything was lit up — very neon — were exactly the way I remembered it.

One has to understand that Japan — even the Tokyo Airport— has a very distinctive look and feel. First off, the various airport employees are immaculately dressed and run around doing their work as if they are robots. And the airport is filled with a strong smell of Japanese food, which I still enjoy. The sights and smells inspired me to buy a beef bowl rice, a bottle of Japanese beer, and for dessert, a kind of Japanese candy that is somewhat comparable to eating a breadstick with chocolate on it. I could have purchased dried cuttlefish — squid — a Japanese treat I used to inhale as readily as Americans consume chocolate bars. But I find squid repulsive now; the nasty odor that emanates from cuttlefish makes me want to barf.

While it seemed like Japan hadn't changed at all in the years I had been away, I was cognizant of the fact that I had changed dramatically. Sitting in an airport lounge drinking the Japanese beer I had purchased, I reminded myself that back in the old days, I would never have been able to drink just one. Yet now my conversion was so real that I could drink just one beer and walk away. As a matter of fact, on one occasion when I got up to board my flight to Guam, the bottle was still half-full.

I figure it's only a matter of time before I return to Japan to speak. I actually received an invitation to speak in a city near Akita where there is an approved Marian apparition. Yet the envelope containing the invitation letter was so badly damaged I could not decipher the return address in order to follow up on the invitation.

Certainly, an extended trip to Japan would be the culmination of my so-called Reparation Tour, because it's the one place where I did a lot of damage and have not been able to return and preach the Gospel. Just about everywhere else — California, Pennsylvania, Virginia, West Virginia, and Louisiana — things have long since been reconciled, and I've been able to bring closure. But a presentation in Japan would be a special blessing in that I would be so grateful to make reparation in the place where I hurt so many people.

I have to admit, however, that it might be a little nerve-wracking to go back. I, of course, would wear a priest collar on the flight over and when passing through the customs post, so it would set a "back in black" kind of tone for the trip. And whatever I'm scheduled to do there, I'll probably attempt to extend my stay and return to my old stomping grounds. In particular, I'd love to visit the military installation where I used to live, which might take some doing. But being that I'm now a priest, I imagine I could contact the military chaplain in advance, explain my situation, and see if he could get me a day pass, which is probably very manageable. I would definitely like to go back and say prayers in front of the myriad places where I used to do crazy things. I'd also like to bless the American dependents who live on the base now — to pray that they not end up like I did.

Finally, there's just one other thing I'd like to do in Japan that makes it a more compelling destination for me to visit than ever before. Most people aren't aware of this, but Japan has become an increasingly popular surfing destination, in part because the country's best beaches have long remained untouched by surfers. This is thanks to the language barrier and their relative inaccessibility to the Americans and Australians who make up the bulk of the world's surfing community.

But there's another reason, too. In the 1990s, surfers began to venture to Miyazaki (located on the island of Kyushu) to visit the Sheraton Seagaia Resort's Ocean Dome wave pool, the largest man-made wave pool in the world. Opened in 1993, it was 300 meters long and 100 meters wide and boasted a retractable roof, a faux flame-spitting volcano, crystal-clear 78-degree water, and perfect 10-foot waves, spitting left- and right-handers every two minutes like clockwork. Unfortunately, it closed in 1997, for reasons that remain a mystery to me. While some surfers complained about the strict safety rules and others fretted about the pool's unpadded cement bottom, the most likely reason for the closure was that the Ocean Dome didn't attract enough visitors for it to remain economically viable. (For some reason, the developers chose to spend millions of dollars building the world's greatest wave pool within sight of a glorious beach.)

Nevertheless, in its relatively short five-year history, the Ocean Dome attracted its share of foreign surfers who also took the opportunity to explore the prime surf spots on the eastern side of the island. Today, I might not be able to visit the Ocean Dome, but I can envision myself taking a trip to some awesome Japanese beach, waxing up my board and riding the waves of the Pacific Ocean just like I did when I lived there; only this time, I would do it as a priest. That would make Japan the perfect last stop on my Reparation Tour.

17

SURFER
PRIEST

T HE FIRST TIME I GOT BACK ON A SURFBOARD
following my conversion, I totally sucked! It was 2005,
and not having surfed consistently in more than 15 years, I
was no better than a novice and an out-of-shape one at that.
There's a big difference between surfing when you are 15
years old and as flexible as a monkey and when you are 32 and
have spent most of your adult life behind a desk.

When I was ordained to the priesthood, I automatically
assumed that I would never surf again. It was a sacrifice I was
willing to accept. I expected to be living in landlocked places
where the Marians have Houses in the United States — places
like Stockbridge, Massachusetts, and Steubenville, Ohio — not
exactly hotbeds for surfing! Back then, I didn't envision having
the opportunities to travel — and surf — that I do today.

Perhaps not surprisingly, my inspiration for returning to
surfing came during a trip I made to San Diego to visit a dear
friend whom I had met at Franciscan University. Ironically,
though, it wasn't a day at the beach that got me thinking about
surfing again. I got the itch after watching professionals like
Kelly Slater, Rob Machado, and Karina Petroni (a pro-life pro-
fessional surfer, by the way) on television shows like FUEL
TV's *Fins*. It got me thinking about what I might need to do
to get back into surfing. I needed something to help me get
back in shape after years of studies, drawing upon how surfing
had been my passion as a boy. Plus, since I now traveled all over
the world, I could quite possibly surf in some amazing places.

The first few steps were obvious: Acquire a used longboard and a wetsuit, the latter being a necessity in San Diego,
as California water is *cold* for about eight months of the year.
When I was 15 years old, I rode a 5'10" thruster (three-fin
board). Now at 32, I had to try and relearn my technique using
a nine-foot single fin board. That stunk! Longboards are fun,
but I had memories of riding shortboards and carving all over
the open face of the wave, so riding a longboard felt very
restricting. Yet I had to do it at first.

Needless to say, during my first session of getting reori-
ented to surfing, I got totally worked! Surfing requires you to
be in very good physical condition, and I was not. Part of my

mistake was that since my friend's house is in San Ysidro (right on the border of Tijuana, Mexico), the closest surfing beach is Imperial Beach. And those who surf Imperial Beach know that it can get heavy, huge, and have super powerful waves — not to mention very polluted water. I guess I thought I could start off where I had left off, and, boy, was I wrong.

I had forgotten how much paddling surfing entailed. And because I wasn't physically fit, I could only stay in the water for 30 minutes before I was totally exhausted. It's embarrassing to admit now, but I was so out of breath that I had to rest on the beach for a while before attempting another session. I shouldn't have been surprised, however. In the first few years after I was ordained, I made no effort to stay in the kind of physical condition required to stay out on the waves for any length of time. Now I was paying the price — both physically and emotionally — for my shortcomings. I quickly realized that if I was going to do any serious surfing, I would need to get in shape first. I had the skills to surf — like riding a bike, you never totally forget — but I needed endurance.

As soon as I returned to Steubenville, I began watching surfing videos and reading surfing magazines, all in an effort to get motivated to exercise. I also began riding a skateboard again (for the first time in a long time). Eventually, I got myself a Ripstik. It is vaguely reminiscent of a skateboard except it only has two wheels — one in the front (under the 'nose') and one in the back (under the 'tail') — and an irregularly shaped caster board (or 'deck'). Unlike a skateboard, you propel yourself by twisting your hips to and fro, and you turn by leaning to either your heel or toe side. In this way, it's comparable to surfing and a good substitute when you're away from the beach.

Finally, on top of everything else, I also acquired an Indo Board balance trainer, which consists of an oval-shaped deck on top of a cylindrical roller. An Indo Board requires the rider to use his sense of balance to stay upright and maneuver the deck and roller in a controlled fashion — "in trim." By mimicking the experience of surfing, an Indo Board not only provides a great workout for your legs, it also helps you to perfect your posture, balance, and coordination, while also improving overall core fitness.

Between the skateboard, Ripstik, Indo Board, daily exercise, and better eating habits, it didn't take me long to get into respectable physical condition. So, by the time my hectic schedule permitted me to surf again, I was ready to go. And I'm pleased to report that the next time I went surfing, I was back in action and ready to start carving up the waves again. And, of course, this meant I could start getting shorter boards that you can carve and totally rip on.

Today, I consider myself an intermediate surfer. In the past five years, I've had the opportunity to surf all over the world. Outside of the places I surfed when I was a kid (Virginia, California, Japan), as a priest, I have now had the great blessing of surfing in Oregon, Hawaii, Guam, Grand Cayman, Argentina, Australia, New Zealand, Mexico, and Costa Rica. And, who knows, maybe in the future I'll be able to speak and surf in places like Portugal, Indonesia, American Samoa, Peru, or the Philippines. Pray for surf!

The thing that I'm most grateful for in terms of surfing is that it allows me to get away when I need to take a break from the exhausting schedule I keep. It has also been a way to make new friends, as being out on the waves is a good place to meet some pretty interesting people. One beautiful morning in San Diego, I was paddling out past the breakers when I struck up a conversation with a guy nearby. While we were waiting for the sets to come in, he casually asked me what I do for a living. When I said, "I'm a Catholic priest," his eyes got all big and he said, "No way. I didn't know that priests surfed." We struck up a friendship, so when I go to San Diego now, I get together with him. We go surfing at places like Imperial Beach, Coronado, Lower Trestles, Ocean Beach, and Del Mar.

It probably goes without saying, however, that an extreme sport like surfing is not for the risk adverse. Anyone who has surfed for any length of time will sooner or later face circumstances or situations that present the possibility of a less-than-desirable outcome. It could be anything from a breach of surf etiquette (as when another surfer cuts you off and "drops in on you," forcing you to take a bad fall) to getting caught in a strong rip current, having the board smack you in the face, or even encountering a shark — one with the potential to inflict pain or life-threatening injury.

In my case, most of the surfing injuries I have sustained came about as a result of the local conditions and undersea topography. Hawaii, for example, is one of the more intimidating places I've ever surfed. A lot of it is shallow reef, and the waves can be very punchy, leaving no room for error. You can be surfing strong waves that are six feet high in water that is only three feet deep. So, if you wipe out, the end result is that you get bashed against the reef. That's exactly what happened to me on Oahu. I went out on a rented board (usually pieces of junk!). Before long, I wiped out and in the process smashed both of my feet against the coral. I literally crawled back to the beach. Then, when I returned to my hotel, I soaked my feet in vinegar to treat the various cuts and lacerations — a condition that surfers sometimes refer to as "reef rash."

Yet Hawaii was child's play compared to Guam, which was a *really* intimidating place to surf. The reef there is so shallow that I couldn't even dig my arms deep into the water to paddle out. On that particular day, I remember going down to the beach full of enthusiasm, giddy to have been fortunate enough to borrow a board from one of the local parishioners. I expected to have a thoroughly rewarding experience, but I returned to the place I was staying only being able to claim a few good lefts.

In terms of pure physical pain, however, my experiences in Hawaii and Guam weren't even close to the agony I experienced after unwittingly stepping on a certain sea creature at Coronado Beach in San Diego. I wasn't doing anything out of the ordinary, just walking out into the surf with my board. Then, suddenly, I felt something sharp prick my foot. "This can't be good," I said to myself.

I immediately retreated back to the beach and observed that I had some kind of stinger sticking out of my foot. Instinctively, I pulled it out, leaving a small puncture wound where the stinger had been. At first, I thought that was the end of it. There was a break in the skin but nothing that would keep me from surfing to my heart's content.

I couldn't have been more wrong. Within 15 or 20 minutes, I was in excruciating pain, curled up in the fetal position right there on the beach. A lifeguard spied me from a lifeguard tower. He ambled over and, without even asking what the trouble was, advised that I had been stung by a stingray. It turns out I had been stung by a Round ray, to be exact. He told me that the only effective treatment would be to immerse my foot in very hot water for the next several hours.

How in the world did the lifeguard know what had happened, I wondered? Apparently, getting stung by a stingray is a very common occurrence at Coronado. The lifeguard went on to tell me that he'd been stung on *seven* different occasions. He sympathized with my plight because, for all intents and purposes, he could feel my pain.

He strongly suggested that I take immediate action to minimize my discomfort. He said, "Unless you keep your foot in very hot water, you are going to be in agony for the next three to five hours."

The lifeguard was prophetic. I dragged myself back to the car. Then, with my wetsuit still on, I drove to my best friend's house in San Ysidro where I keep my surfboards, writhing in pain all the while. There, I immersed my foot in hot water, and as soon as I plunged in, I felt instant relief. But whenever I took my foot out, the pain quickly returned, as violent as ever. At one point, I removed my foot from the water to take a bathroom break, only to find I actually had to cut the break short because the pain was so intense.

Needless to say, that stingray taught me a harsh lesson. Nowadays, I always make sure to do the "stingray shuffle." This involves shuffling your feet along the ocean floor as you walk out in the water. By kicking up sand, you serve notice that you are coming, so it gives stingrays the opportunity to scurry away before you step on them. Like everyone else, I might look a little silly shuffling my feet as I wade into the surf, but now I do it every time.

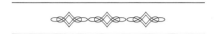

While stepping on a stingray was exquisitely painful, the most downright frightening experience I've ever had was surfing amongst leopard sharks for the first time. Even though leopard sharks don't present much danger — at least not to humans — surfing in the midst of dozens of six-foot sharks can be more than a little disconcerting. Imagine gliding over five feet of crystal clear water. Then, when you look down, all you see are long, slender, silver and black sharks. "They won't bother you; they are bottom feeders," is what everyone says. Of course, that doesn't change the fact that you have to be careful about how and where you dismount. Otherwise, you could fall in the wrong place and come down on one of them.

The first time I surfed with leopard sharks, I was all by myself surfing the dawn patrol. It's always kind of scary being by yourself out in the water in the early morning when there is no one around. But I totally freaked out when all the sudden, I saw a six-foot shadow pass right under me — then another one, then another one. I thought I was surrounded by man-eaters and about to be breakfast. I paddled to shore as fast as I could, only to be told by a local arriving on the scene that they were relatively harmless, so I had nothing to worry about.

Meanwhile, the other thing that really freaks me out is surfing in dark water. At least in clear water, it's possible to see a shark — or a dolphin or seal — coming. But when you're in 10 feet of water and can't see what's below you — *can't even see your own feet* — that's just plain spooky. Luckily, in most of the places I've surfed, the water has been clear. But whenever the water is dark, it's particularly unnerving for me. Even if it's just a seal swimming up close (and that has happened many, many times), it's still startling because you don't know it's a seal, at least until it's too late to do anything about it.

Having said all that, I don't think *any* sea creature could possibly keep me from surfing. Sure, in places like Australia, I'm nervous about the possibility of encountering Great White sharks, box jellyfish, Taipan snakes, and all the other potentially life-threatening organisms found in the waters Down Under. But I wouldn't let them prevent me from going out on my board.

That's because in my mind there's almost no greater thrill than riding a wave, especially early in the morning when the sea looks like glass. There's just nothing like dropping in on a perfectly peeling 6-to-8-foot A-frame wave. I'm a goofy foot, which means I stand with my left foot in back — as opposed to regular stance, with left in front. At San Diego beaches like Del Mar or Imperial Beach, a goofy footer like myself can go left all day.

I also especially enjoy surfing at dawn because there aren't many other surfers out that early in the morning. You have to be hardcore to wake up at 5:30 a.m. and jump into 53 degree water. I just love it though. As weird as it sounds, there is also something very mystical about surfing in a light rain. The water all around you sizzles, and all your senses are alive. It's just awesome to be alive.

For me, though, surfing provides a number of tangible benefits that extend beyond the joy of riding the waves. As one might expect, the seven-day-a-week work schedule of a priest isn't necessarily conducive to good health, as there isn't much time for regular physical activity. In my case, surfing has helped me manifest a physically healthy priesthood — not so much because of the surfing itself — but because I am always making time to work out, trying to stay fit in anticipation of my next surfing trip. I want to have the stamina to stay in the water for four to five hours or more on those rare occasions when the opportunity presents itself.

Perhaps more importantly, I find that there's also a spiritual dimension to surfing. I like to say that Jesus was a surfer because he walked on water. And when I'm surfing, I always get the sense that there is something almost supernatural going on. In fact, St. Faustina in her *Diary* frequently speaks of plunging into "the ocean of God's mercy." Well, in my case, I'm surfing on its waters, experiencing God's goodness, His love and mercy.

Think about it. When you're surfing, you are not doing your own will. You are simply participating in something that was there before you were, and it continues to occur whether you are there or not. All you can do is ride the waves, not manipulate them or control them. You are allowing yourself to be taken by the water, although the better you are able to ride the waves, the more you get stoked. In my opinion, no sport provides more of a feeling of joy. When I go surfing, I get so pumped that I sometimes find it difficult to come out of the water. I could stay there forever.

Of course, I'm not the only one to observe that surfing can be an almost mystical experience. I recently finished reading a book titled *I Surf, Therefore I Am: A Philosophy of Surfing* by Catholic philosopher and theologian Peter Kreeft. In the book, he gives the reader philosophical reasons why surfing is simply one of the best things you can do on earth — and I tend to agree with him. Outside of God, surfing is the most enjoyable thing I do, and I'm seriously hoping to surf in God for all eternity, in His ocean of mercy.

18

ONGOING
CONVERSION

Shortly after my parents converted to Catholicism, my mother began praying for me. Day and night she prayed that her incorrigible first-born son would change his wicked ways, embrace the Catholic faith, and begin leading a holy life. She must have been a very strong woman because, for the longest time, it seemed that her prayers were in vain. Weeks turned into months, months turned into years, and still I evinced no indication that I would ever change. Not only did I continue my blasphemous and immoral behavior, I openly rejected Catholicism, mocking the "foolish" prayers my family stopped to say before meals and dismissing my mother's request to accompany the family to church on Sunday.

Yet my mother's faith was unwavering. Thanks to *her* own conversion experience, she knew the power and mercy of God. And she knew change was possible in God's time. So she continued to pray for me daily, even going so far as to plant prayer cards in my bedroom and in my clothes. I would come home wasted after a night of partying. Then, when I would lie down, I would feel something — it felt like a dollar — under my pillow. I would pull it out, and it would be a prayer card with St. Michael the Archangel on it. Or I would reach into my pants' pocket. And instead of finding money there, I would discover a coin-type thing that read: "Mary, conceived without sin, pray for us."

Although I didn't even know what prayer cards were at the time, my reaction was predictable.

"Whatever."

But my mother would become my spiritual hero. She continued planting these little bugs in an attempt to change my life. Today, she likes to say that she always saw the good in me, even when I was bad to the bone. She was convinced that things would eventually work out.

As you know by now, things *have* worked out, better than anyone in the Calloway family could have possibly imagined. These days, my mother feels like the happiest woman on the face of the earth. Not only does she remain very much in love with her husband — my dad — she is as proud of me as a mother can be. She is constantly affirming me and telling me how much she loves me.

Naturally, much of my mother's peace of mind has come as a result of my becoming a Marian priest. When I joined the Marian community, she was delighted — no, *thrilled* — because she saw a change in me that was so real. Afterwards, we became very close. And ever since, we've been able to talk about anything.

I know the moment in time when our relationship changed, too. It happened when we began to pray together. It's so amazing to be able to sit down with your mom and pray a Rosary. And I feel the same way today. It gives me such a sense of peace to pray with her and to know the joy of finally giving my mother some peace. I tell her I love her and relish the fact that she doesn't need to worry about me any more.

It gives me great joy to know my mother's heart is at peace. She doesn't have to worry about me for one single moment ever again. I want to give her that peace.

That's why my message to mothers who have suffered a maternal-broken heart is a message of hope. Know that there is always hope that God can change things. The change may not come immediately, but if you persevere and love like my mother did, things can and do change for the better. After all, the tears of a mother are powerful before God. And if you persevere, the joy that you experience when you help give spiritual birth to a son or daughter will be incomprehensible — just like my mother's joy.

By now, you're probably wondering why I haven't included my stepfather as part of this conversation. In all honesty, I don't even consider him my stepfather at all. He is a real father to me, and I love him dearly. The reason I have not mentioned him too much so far is because he deserves special mention here. As you might expect, in much the same way that people familiar with my conversion story ask about my mother, they also inquire about how my dad is doing. They usually phrase the question along the lines of: "Your father must be a great guy to have adopted you, to have put up with all your mischief, and paid the bills for all the damage you caused."

Those people are right on target. My dad is a great guy, and I always stress that he is an amazing husband for my mother, with whom he remains very much in love. And today he, too, continues to be very much committed to the Church. Actually, both of my parents are very involved in their church.

As for my brother Matthew, when I joined the Marians, I struggled mightily with feelings of guilt about leaving him, lamenting the fact that he wouldn't have an older brother to play with and grow up with. Leaving Matthew was one of the hardest things I've done in my whole life. I prayed to God about my decision, saying, "God, I know you are calling me to the priesthood, yet leaving Matthew is extremely painful. You have to take care of him because I am not going to be able to do it."

Matthew simply means the world to me. I have a difficult time describing why it is that way. But one of the analogies I use is that Jesus is my brother and He has such a love for me that He was willing to die for me. In that separation, He was willing to go all the way, so I could now be with Him for all eternity. That's how I feel about the love for my brother. I would do anything for him, and I love him so much that I would give my life for him. And in some sense, I am.

For me personally, one final thing I feel compelled to emphasize is that my conversion experience is ongoing. Just as I needed my mother's prayers to help me find my faith, I continue to need *your* prayers as I go through my ongoing purification.

I remind people of this because often when telling my conversion story, I get the impression that people think I have arrived, as in, "You're a saint! You're so holy!" I think it's because the Protestant mentality of "You're saved!" has crept into the Catholic understanding of conversion. This explains why some people view my conversion experience as a one-time event.

But the experience I had back in 1992 was merely an *initial* experience, only one among many. And the conversion experiences that I've had — and continue to have — are in some ways even more amazing than that initial experience. Why? Because I have to cooperate with God's grace and learn to die to my selfish interests. When I had my initial conversion, it was almost like a honeymoon. God romanced me and took me into the bridal chamber. But afterwards, as time went on, the honeymoon ended. The relationship became more akin to a daily marriage between God and my soul. Today, it's an ongoing choice to continue to be converted and undergo the process of learning to love as God loves.

It's especially important that young people understand the nature of my conversion experience. I've had many teenagers approach me — I love them for their boldness — and say things like, "Father Calloway, I'm not gonna change my behavior. I want to enjoy all the experiences that you enjoyed in your youth. Then I'll have my conversion experience, and I'll be good to go. Just like you."

I always say, "No, you don't understand. You shouldn't play with fire like that." On one hand, I understand why young people think that way. I would have probably said the exact same thing. But their approach presumes that conversion is a one-time event when, in fact, it is alive and ongoing.

I encourage young people who feel like they might be at a crossroads to think deeply and ask questions like: Why are you on this earth? What is your purpose in life? Do you believe there is more to life than maintaining your daily existence? If you listen, your heart will tell you that there *has to be more,* because you long for it. I encourage you to learn how to pray and to allow yourself to experience conversion.

Further, if you happen to come from a screwed-up background — if you believe your past is so wicked that it would never be possible for you to experience conversion (or, like myself, become a priest) — I'm living proof that God can make remarkable things happen. I'm certainly not unique either. I have met so many people who are undergoing conversion, and they come from all walks of life. Perhaps their sinful lives may not have been as crazy as mine — their past lives not as sordid — but they have emerged from the same cultural wasteland that I did.

And you know what? The fact that they have come through these experiences is good for others. It's beneficial in terms of their interaction with people they meet. For example, many of the young priests I know (not to mention the Marian seminarians who are currently in formation) have spent many years of their lives out in the world and now know how to communicate the Gospel message to a world that desperately needs to hear it.

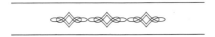

I want to be a saint — like a shark to meat, I want it bad — but I'm not there yet. As I alluded to earlier, when I experienced my conversion, I got hit with the Divine 2 x 4. God nailed me — hard.

Yet the process of becoming a saint is not a lollipop experience where all you taste is sweet sugar. Yes, God romances the soul for a time, but eventually He takes the lollipop away and wants the person to cooperate with all the things He is going to allow that person to experience.

There's an ancient monastic axiom that states, "The ways a man sins are the ways that a man will be purified." So am I tempted now? Yes. I'm not an angel. Do I struggle with my weaknesses? Yeah, I do. But this is allowed by God because, in the midst of temptations and struggles, I have to choose to love Him each and every day.

So it's a little overwhelming sometimes when people approach me and insist that I am holy or ask if they are permitted to touch me. Of course, some cultures have very demonstrative means of showing reverence for clergy. For instance, when Filipinos encounter a priest, they get down on one knee and put his hand on their forehead. But what I'm talking about is a little different. People will actually come up to me and ask, "Can we touch you?"

I always shake my head and think, "Good grief. I'm not God."

At the same time, I understand that everyone wants a hero. I want one, too. And I understand that from their perspective, what has happened to me is amazing. Certainly, I don't mind it in the sense that some people need to see and experience something powerful. If my conversion story does it for them, that's incredible. But I always make sure to remind people that I am not a relic. I haven't been canonized yet. In fact, I still have a long, long way to go.

So, once again, I urge you all to pray for me. I want to be holy, but it's a spiritual battle. And I promise to pray for all those who read this book. I totally know that even for those who strive for holiness — even in the lives of saints — you find great temptations and struggles. It's all because God is a Father and doesn't want us to be covered with grace as though we really are nothing more than a pile of dung. On the contrary! He wants to transform us from within, so that we become His children and pattern ourselves on the imitation of Christ, which is sacrificial love unto death. He wants us to say, "I will obey You because I love You, even to the point of giving my life. Jesus, I trust in You!"

Sanctity is what we were put on this earth for. Some days I don't do a good job, and I thank God so much for confession. I admit that I have to avail myself of confession — a lot. And I'm sure that if you heard my confessions, you would, most certainly, be praying for me.

But you know what? I'm glad that I'm still in the process of becoming holy, striving for sanctity, and being purified. It shows that God loves me and holds me in such worth that He wants me to cooperate and surrender and go through this purifying fire. I know that I can only be purified if I go through fire.

So this is by no means the end of my story. It's continuing. And I need your prayers to help me continue to be faithful to the end. Remember that I'm not the Messiah and I'm not an angel. I'm just here to bring other people to God. I need Him as much as anybody else.

And there's *No Turning Back*!

I truly believe in the depths of my heart and soul that our Jesus, The Divine Mercy, and our Immaculate Mother Mary have and will continue to light the paths that you take on each new journey of bringing Jesus to the world.

In teaching and inspiring all people with the true gifts and Sacraments of our faith, you refresh and remind us that we are all called to be disciples of mercy to each other.

May the Holy Trinity inspire you to forge ahead with humility and deepened trust in our Lord's divine providence.

The Marians of the Immaculate Conception, zealous men, are truly witnessing to Jesus' Divine Mercy.

Our Lady gave her unconditional 'yes,' teaching us to be unwavering in our love, completely faithful, and always trusting in Jesus.

So awesome to be able to go to your website, Fr. Donnie, and know that we can help you spread the good news to help save souls for Jesus Christ, the Way, the Truth, and the Life.

God, I love the boy who became a man ordained by mercy and grace to do God's will!

Let's all pray our Rosary for our priests and religious.

Keep the pics coming; love the surfing pics. Too cool!

Love & Peace,
Mom

Little Donnie.

My Days of Innocence.

Early life in West Virginia
with Mom.

Mom, my cousin Matt Bianco, and me.

Inseparable mother and son.

Birthday 1982.

School picture from Virginia Beach when things started to go bad.

My brother Matt and I at our house in San Diego.

Early days in Japan.

Outside our house in Atsugi, Japan.

With my dad after my first rehab in Pennsylvania.

Contemplating the waves on Virginia Beach.

The Deadhead years
(photo taken by Brian Beshears).

Christmas cash for
a dark soul.

Post-conversion photo. The National Shrine of
The Divine Mercy, Stockbridge, Massachusetts.

On vacation from seminary visiting my mom.

My first trip to Rome. September 1997.

Trip home for my brother's high school graduation.

Ordination to the priesthood at the National Shrine
of The Divine Mercy in Stockbridge, Massachusetts. May 31, 2003.

Ordination
day joy!

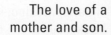

The love of a
mother and son.

My beautiful
mother.

Mom and Dad at
Christmas time.

At my best friend's house
in San Ysidro, California.
Tijuana, Mexico, is in the
background.

New surfboard
ready to rip!

Sunset Cliffs,
California.

Cold California Surf.

Surfing at Del Mar, California.

Co-hosting Divine Mercy Sunday for EWTN with Fr. Joe Roesch, MIC.
There were approximately 18,000 people in attendance at
the National Shrine of The Divine Mercy in Stockbridge,
Massachusetts. April 19, 2009.

PROMOTING DIVINE MERCY SINCE 1941

Marian Press, the publishing apostolate of the Marian Fathers of the Immaculate Conception of the B.V.M., has published and distributed millions of religious books, magazines, and pamphlets that teach, encourage, and edify Catholics around the world. Our publications promote and support the ministry and spirituality of the Marians worldwide. Loyal to the Holy Father and to the teachings of the Catholic Church, the Marians fulfill their special mission by:

- Fostering devotion to Mary, the Immaculate Conception.

- Promoting The Divine Mercy message and devotion.

- Offering assistance to the dying and the deceased, especially the victims of war and disease.

- Promoting Christian knowledge, administering parishes, shrines, and conducting missions.

Based in Stockbridge, Mass, Marian Press is known as the publisher of the *Diary of Saint Maria Faustina Kowalska,* and the Marians are the leading authorities on The Divine Mercy message and devotion.

Stockbridge is also the home of the National Shrine of The Divine Mercy, the Association of Marian Helpers, and a destination for thousands of pilgrims each year.

Globally, the Marians' ministries also include missions in developing countries where the spiritual and material needs are enormous.

To learn more about the Marians, their spirituality, publications or ministries, visit **marian.org** or **thedivinemercy.org**, the Marians' website that is devoted exclusively to Divine Mercy.

Below is a view of the National Shrine of The Divine Mercy and its Residence in Stockbridge, Mass. The Shrine, which was built in the 1950s was declared a National Shrine by the National Conference of Catholic Bishops on March 20, 1996.

© MARIE ROMAGNANO

MARIAN PRESS
STOCKBRIDGE · MA 01263

For our complete line of books, DVDs, CDs, and other trustworthy resources on Divine Mercy and Mary, visit thedivinemercy.org or call 1-800-462-7426 to have our latest catalog sent to you.

BOOKS BY FR. DONALD

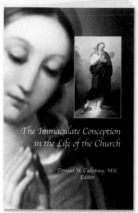

ICLC 9781932773934

THE IMMACULATE CONCEPTION IN THE LIFE OF THE CHURCH

In 2004, Fr. Donald edited his first book, *The Immaculate Conception in the Life of the Church*. This collection of essays came from a symposium on the Immaculate Conception for the 150th anniversary of the proclamation of the dogma. Paperback. 198 pages.

THE VIRGIN MARY AND THEOLOGY OF THE BODY

In these brilliant essays, prominent experts explore how Pope John Paul II's groundbreaking *Theology of the Body* applies to the Blessed Virgin Mary. Edited by Donald H. Calloway, MIC. Paperback. 285 pages.

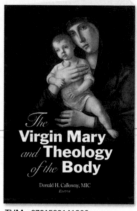

TVM 9781596141360

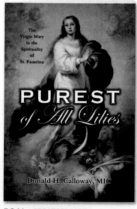

POAL 9781596141957

PUREST OF ALL LILIES: THE VIRGIN MARY IN THE SPIRITUALITY OF ST. FAUSTINA

This was the first book written completely by Fr. Donald. "It's basically my licentiate thesis on St. Faustina and the Virgin Mary," he explains. "It was edited to keep it from being too technical for a general audience." The book explores St. Faustina's rich relationship with the Mother of God, as recorded in the saint's *Diary*. Father Donald discusses the important lessons the Blessed Mother taught St. Faustina about suffering, purity of heart, and humility. He also includes an analysis of St. Faustina's poems that often use flower metaphors for Mary. Paperback. 128 pages.

To order call 1-800-462-7426 or visit thedivinemercy.org

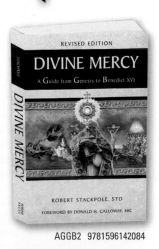

ESSENTIAL DIVINE MERCY RESOURCES

The Divine Mercy

Message and Devotion

THE DIVINE MERCY MESSAGE AND DEVOTION

Fr. Seraphim Michalenko, MIC with Vinny Flynn and Robert Stackpole

This booklet provides an overview to one of the Catholic Church's fastest growing movements. All elements and prayers of the message and devotion are included in an easy-to-follow format. Paperback. 88 pages.

English 3.5" x 6"   9780944203583
Large Print 5" x 7.5" 9780944203477
Spanish 3.5" x 6"   9780944203767

DISCOVER THE MANDATE

Pope Benedict's Divine Mercy Mandate is brilliantly written. David Came traces the thread of Divine Mercy throughout the papacy of Benedict XVI and pulls back the veil on a papal program for what it means to "go forth and be witnesses of God's mercy." This is a must-read.

— Drew Mariani, Nationally syndicated radio talk show host, author, and award-winning journalist

Paperback • 159 pages
PBBK 9781596142039

Rachel, Weep No More

How Divine Mercy Heals the Effects of Abortion

Bryan Thatcher, MD, & Fr. Frank Pavone

RWNM 9780944203835

RACHEL WEEP NO MORE: HOW DIVINE MERCY HEALS THE EFFECTS OF ABORTION

Bryan Thatcher and Fr. Frank Pavone

This booklet is a great source of hope for anyone who has been involved with abortion because it provides a plan for cutting through the pain and the lies, acknowledging the truth, and receiving God's powerful healing from the effects of this tragedy. Norma McCorvey (formerly "Jane Roe" of Roe vs. Wade) and Bernard Nathanson, formerly a leader in the abortion industry, both share their amazing stories about getting out of the culture of death.

To order call 1-800-462-7426 or visit thedivinemercy.org